PARTY DYNAMICS

PARTY DYNAMICS

*The Democratic Coalition
and the Politics of Change*

RICHARD L. RUBIN
COLUMBIA UNIVERSITY

New York
OXFORD UNIVERSITY PRESS
1976

To Len, my wife and best friend.

Acknowledgments

There have been many who generously provided their assistance in the preparation of this book, and the debts should be acknowledged. My deep appreciation goes first to Demetrios Caraley and Charles V. Hamilton, who were both involved from the inception of this research to the final literary product. Their valuable criticism and encouragement cannot be overestimated. Other colleagues at Columbia and Barnard have also given valuable help in improving the manuscript, and thanks are owed to Bruce L. R. Smith, Harvey C. Mansfield, Richard M. Pious, and Gerald B. Finch for their constructive criticism.

I am also grateful to scholars at other universities who provided valuable suggestions at various stages of the manuscript. To Duane Lockard at Princeton University, Everett Carll Ladd, Jr., at the University of Connecticut, and Ira Katznelson at the University of Chicago, I owe thanks for their interest and criticism.

Substantial amounts of data were made available through the cooperation of Louis Harris Associates, the Inter-University Consortium for Political Research, and the Roper Public Opinion Research Center. In addition, various studies done by CBS Survey and

Data Services were made available through the cooperation of Warren I. Mitofsky, Director.

An expression of thanks is owed to my editor at Oxford, Nancy Lane, for her continuous efforts in behalf of the manuscript, to Sam Kachigan for valuable technical help, and to Pauline Chapman, my typist, for her cooperation.

All of the individuals noted above have helped in the preparation of this manuscript, but naturally the author alone should be held accountable for what is written. I personally accept all responsibility for the material and interpretation expressed herein.

R.L.R.

New York
January 1976

Contents

PARTY DYNAMICS

Introduction

Repeated surveys of American public opinion have shown that for many years a wide margin of voters have considered themselves Democrats rather than Republicans—and yet the Democratic Party's presidential candidates have not been able to win a majority of the presidential elections held in the last three decades. Heightening this seeming paradox is the Democratic success in winning party control of Congress which, with the exception of two very brief periods, has been maintained by the Democrats since 1932. This situation exacerbates the division of governmental power by politically insulating Congress and the President from each other's electoral fortunes, frequently leaving them in the hands of opposing parties, and permitting each party to avoid clear responsibility for emergent public policies.

This book will focus primarily on the growing instability of the Democratic presidential coalition, a condition which has prevented joint control of national policy, and will seek to explain the decline in the power and consistency of the majority coalition. The Democratic coalition has long served, as V. O. Key often noted, as the popular underpinning for much of the innovation and change in

American politics since the Depression. However, its presidential voice has grown weak and unsteady. Even the victories that may result from a combination of Watergate and, more importantly, a major economic recession are unlikely to provide a durable advantage for the Democratic presidential party, for unreconciled long-term socio-economic and racial forces have been weakening the Democratic coalition persistently since the end of World War II.

Although the dramatic rise of "Independents" (who substantially outnumbered Republicans by the mid-1970s) has shrunk the number of declared partisans overall, much Democratic failure at the polls can be attributed to the inability of the Democratic presidential candidates to keep their traditional supporters behind them. In 1972, for example, Senator George McGovern received only 46 percent of the Catholic vote and 48 percent of the labor union vote—the first time since the New Deal that these two key electoral groups supported a Republican over a Democratic presidential candidate.

While much of the blame for the loss of these key Democratic groups has been attributed to McGovern's poor campaign in 1972, McGovern's candidacy can only share the responsibility for losses among Catholics and organized labor, since the support of these core groups of the New Deal realignment has been weakening for over two decades. Complicating the matter of internal stability for the Democrats, these traditionally Democratic interests have become uncertain party supporters just as new electoral groups, such as Blacks, have become important and consistent contributors to the changing party coalition (about one-fifth of all Democratic votes in 1968 and 1972), with competing claims of their own on the party.

Samuel Lubell has described in his classic *The Future of American Politics* how the process of political change seems always to be focused on elements interacting within the majority coalition (the "Sun" party, as he described it), suggesting that the "key to the political warfare of any particular period will be found among the clashing elements in the majority party."[1] As each new majority party "Sun" ascends, it brings with it, according to Lubell, its own eventual opposition, and as it fights out the issues of its time, this opposition must be reasonably reconciled or contained. If it is not absorbed, the majority "Sun" becomes the minority "Moon" party, losing the political initiative to a new majority party until future failures create fresh opportunities for it to regain party dominance. While some critics see external social and political events rather than internal conflict as the *originating* causes of the disintegration of the majority "Sun," Lubell and his critics as well agree that, whatever the causes of political conflict, they are eventually *played out* first in the conflict of different groups in the majority party.[2]

The major social and political forces of an era thus press upon the dominant party—at present a faltering Democratic "Sun"—to meet new needs and adjust itself to new social and political realities. But by its meeting these very needs for social and political change, old relationships are disrupted and the tenuous agreements among potentially competitive interests within the party are seriously weakened. The need to accommodate the future seems, almost of necessity, to destabilize past relationships, and attempts to reconcile divergent socio-political forces appear to stimulate new internal dynamics that threaten the very stability of the original party coalition.

One need only compare the different arenas of conflict at the national conventions of the two major parties in 1968 and 1972 to

1. Samuel Lubell, *The Future of American Politics* (2nd ed., revised. Garden City: Doubleday, 1955), p. 217.
2. While accepting most of Lubell's analysis, Everett Ladd, Jr., makes a valid objection to Lubell's suggestion that the causes of a new political era (the coming of a new majority party "Sun") originate from the conflict of supporters already in the majority coalition. It is "not the new majority party that brings 'its own orbit of conflict' but rather a new 'orbit of conflict' which often requires a new majority party." See Everett Ladd, Jr., *American Political Parties: Social Changes and Political Response* (New York: W. W. Norton, 1970), p. 4.

see the merit of Lubell's thesis that the major conflicts of socio-political change are fought out first in the dominant party. At both Democratic conventions, significant numbers of activists representing the anti-war movement, Blacks, party reformers, labor interests, and established local party organizations all contested with fervor and skill to shape the Democratic Party, while the Republican conventions showed hardly a test trace of these divergent and dynamic forces in American politics.[3]

In order to understand better the questions of change in American politics, this study focuses on developments in the majority party since the end of World War II, examining the dynamic forces of the past and present that seek to influence the majority party and, consequently, shape America's political future. Can the Democratic Party regain its presidential dominance? Can it successfully integrate new claimants with old supporters? Is it capable of successfully balancing the desire for innovation and change with the need for stability and continuity in American politics?

To find answers to these questions, we will analyze the majority party at both mass and elite levels, as we seek to uncover new linkages among the mass electorate, party activists, and political change. In Part I the voting behavior of key urban support groups, the bastions of earlier Democratic successes, will be analyzed in the context of two massive migrations of Americans that, like most migratory waves, have had major destabilizing effects on existing social and political cleavages. In the first, millions of Southern Blacks, primarily rural in origin, have journeyed to the old cities of the North, particularly to the large cities in the East and Midwest—a massive influx that has made racial polarity no longer just a Southern political dimension but a national one as well. In the second wave, the migration of huge numbers of Whites to the

3. Divisive conflict also occurs in the minority "Moon" coalition, e.g., the 1964 Goldwater nomination, but not the same kind of conflict. In 1964 the groups involved were established factions fighting for dominance and did not involve new claimants for change. See John Kessel, *The Gold-Water Coalition: Republican Strategies in 1964* (Indianapolis: Bobbs-Merrill, 1968), pp. 25–58.

suburban fringes of these densely populated great cities has provided major socio-political challenges to a party whose strength was based to a great extent upon White urban supporters. Not only has the composition of the urban population changed drastically in these Northern cities in only a few decades, but vital sources of potential Democratic electoral strength—Catholics, labor unionists, and other people of the great cities—have left the environment of their political origins for a new and different life-style in the suburbs. Part I will be, in effect, an extensive analysis of political change among the traditionally supportive urban groups of the old Democratic coalition in the context of rapidly changing cities and suburbs.

In Part II, the impact of changing support among these critical groups of the Democratic coalition will be followed into the intra-party political arena, particularly into leadership and activist conflict in national nomination politics. Here the focus will fall heavily upon the internal party battles between certain key factions of the Democratic Party as changes in traditional group support in the mass electorate are translated into efforts by new political activists to gain control of the principal resource of American party power—the presidential nomination. It is in this battle to select the party's candidate that the various competing elements clash most vividly for power, for in the absence of any strong national party apparatus to seize, genuine intra-party power is primarily gained by shaping the choice of the party's presidential nominee.

Since the early 1960s, racial interests, anti-war insurgents, party reformers, and other political forces have sought with increasing determination to express themselves through the Democratic Party, often creating as a result conflict with leaders of local party organizations (the "machines"), labor union leaders, and other elites of past party dominance. It was, in fact, the inability of these various new and old factions to reconcile their interests effectively after the divisive nominating campaigns of 1968 and 1972 that made successful campaigns in the November elections extremely difficult for the Democratic nominees. The high political costs of intra-party conflict in the nominations of Hubert Humphrey and George McGovern had greatly increased the odds against victory for them in the subsequent general elections.

Part II is not, however, simply a study of factionalism in the national party organization, particularly in view of the decentralized nature of power in the national party itself. Rather it is a study of the dynamics of party conflict *as the party organizes* to select a presidential leader every four years in the context of 1) changing support by certain key groups in the electorate, 2) increasing ideological and racial claims by different Democratic elites, and 3) the increased capability of insurgents to challenge party organizational authority—all of which have combined to increase substantially the extent of internal conflict over who shall select the Democratic nominee and shape the national face of the party.

Following the analysis of the specific internal dynamics of a faltering majority party, Part III will compare and contrast the nature of the two rather distinct arenas of presidential candidacy— the intra-party and inter-party universes—in order to assess the changing shape and dynamics of conflict in the American electorate. What changes have occurred in the relationships among various activists seeking political influence in the Democratic Party? What new dynamics have affected the linkage between these competitive party elites and party rank and file? And as the intensity and scope of conflict rapidly broaden *within* the majority party, how do these changes affect the American electorate and the American party system as a whole? In brief, Part III seeks to clarify at least some of the critical relationships between electoral *cores* and party *corps* as they interact first in the choice of a presidential candidate and then again in reappraisal of their handiwork in the November general election.

I

The Urban Coalition in the Suburban Era

I

Democrats and
the Changing Metropolis

In less than a century, the United States has witnessed major waves of migration that have significantly altered the physical, social, and political patterns of the country. Beginning in the last quarter of the nineteenth century, an accelerating and relentless explosion of the big city population developed as migrants were drawn from the small towns and farms and from foreign lands by a surge of industrial development. By 1920 the first phase of massive metropolitan population movement was statistically clear—more Americans lived in cities than in rural areas.

The force of industrial development and the process of urbanization were responsible for profound modifications in the old sectional basis of the party system in America—as the Democratic Party, long dominated by the agrarian South, also became the party of the great cities of the North. The urbanizing process of America had, in fact, laid the groundwork for party cleavages more along class lines than the earlier sectional alignment, as urbanization helped to shape new kinds of Democrats and Republicans.[1]

1. V. O. Key, Jr., *Politics, Parties and Pressure Groups* (5th ed., New York: Thomas Y. Crowell, 1964), p. 249.

The development and eventual solidification of the urban vote in the East and Midwest became the single most important component in the evolution of the New Deal and post-New Deal coalition. But although the cities of these regions did eventually become the key bastions of national Democratic Party support, the shift of the urban masses to the Democrats was not simply a change produced by the economic chaos of the Great Depression. It was, rather, a shift occurring in distinct phases. In fact, even before the economic debacle of the depression years, Northern Catholics, making up the largest single segment of the electorate in the big industrial states, were moving in great numbers into the Democratic Party, while the Republican Party was simultaneously becoming more dependent on rural and small-town Protestant support.[2]

In 1928, the Democratic nomination of Al Smith, a Catholic, had deepened this religious support and brought further significant changes in the traditional presidential coalition. Republican Herbert Hoover carried 200 Southern counties in the election of 1928 that had never before gone Republican, while Democrat Al Smith swung 122 new Northern counties to the Democratic column. In the twelve largest cities in America, the religious factor helped change a Republican plurality of over 1,250,000 in 1924 into a Democratic plurality of 38,000 in 1928, a remarkable switch to the Democrats in the light of the huge 1928 Republican landslide.[3]

While the election of 1928 increased and solidified the predominantly Catholic working-class affinity for the Democratic Party of the North, it was not until eight years later that Protestant workers joined their Catholic co-workers politically along *class* lines. Even the first phase of the Depression (1929 to 1932) was not sufficient to shake the traditional allegiance of Northern Protestant workers to the Republican Party. It was, in fact, only after the political activity of the first Roosevelt administration that urban

2. V. O. Key, Jr., "A Theory of Critical Elections," *Journal of Politics,* 17 (1955) 3–18.
3. Samuel Lubell, *The Future of American Politics* (2nd ed., Garden City, New York: Doubleday, 1955), p. 37.

working-class support solidified across religious lines so that by 1936 working-class and Catholic support could supply the largest part of a 3,608,000 plurality for the Democratic candidate from the vote in just twelve large cities.[4]

The Roosevelt coalition of the 1930s and the early 1940s had succeeded in welding together two important and uneasy allies into an electoral foundation for presidential victory. The thirteen one-party Southern states, long the agrarian base of the Democratic Party, joined with the large urban-industrial states and provided the essential electoral basis for four presidential victories from 1932 to 1944. In the Northern segment of the coalition, Catholics and rapidly organizing workers formed a solid Democratic base in the cities and gave the Democrats the winning margins in the heavily industrial states, while in the Southern segment, historically one-party politics and the suppression of racial issues combined to give huge Democratic majorities.

The solidarity of this electoral alliance of the urban North and the rural South began to weaken after the election of Franklin Roosevelt for his fourth term in 1944, and an increasing dependency of the Democrats on the Northern urbanized states resulted from this decline in the support of the "solid South." The thirteen Southern states that gave all their 148 electoral votes to Roosevelt in 1944 (only 216 electoral votes in all were needed to win) gave Hubert Humphrey in 1968 only the 25 electoral votes of Texas, in a closely contested election, and gave none to McGovern in the 1972 Nixon landslide.

Beginning with the defection of Strom Thurmond's States' Rights candidacy in 1948 (39 electoral votes in five Southern states), the Southern contribution to the Democratic coalition clearly began to erode, the Democratic candidate getting the majority of Southern electoral votes in only three of the six presidential elections from 1952 to 1972 and, importantly, practically no support in the last two of these six contests.

4. *Ibid.*

As the South rapidly declined as a source of Democratic strength after World War II, the urbanized North became both its most important base and a pivotal battleground for Democratic presidential victories. In 1960 the eleven most urbanized states of the East and Midwest,[5] states that house the principal Catholic and union populations in the country, gave 168 of their 218 electoral votes to John F. Kennedy, and even in Hubert Humphrey's losing effort in 1968 these states still provided a majority of their votes for the Democratic candidate. The Eastern part of this eleven-state "urban belt," casting 102 of its 126 electoral votes for Humphrey, became the Democratic bastion, while the heavily urbanized Midwestern states became the swing states in close elections; their vote provided the Democrats either with victory, as in 1960, or with defeat, as in 1968.[6]

But just as the massive urban migrations destabilized political alignments in the late nineteenth century and the early decades of the twentieth century, so two new massive shifts of American population have once again introduced new social and economic dynamics, dynamics that threaten the strength of the Democratic Party in its remaining metropolitan strongholds of the Northeast and Midwest. First, the northward migration by Southern Blacks, relatively slow in the Depression years, accelerated rapidly in the 1940s, 50s, and 60s, as economic and social opportunities in the North broadened for Black Americans. Whereas on the eve of World War II more than three-quarters of all American Blacks lived in the South, three decades later only half lived there, the result of out-migration averaging more than 150,000 Blacks each year.[7]

5. In the East: New York, Connecticut, Massachusetts, Pennsylvania, Rhode Island, and New Jersey. In the Midwest: Michigan, Illinois, Indiana, Wisconsin, and Ohio.
6. In the West both the Mountain and Pacific sub-regions have contributed large majorities to Republican presidential candidates in all elections between 1952 and 1972—with the only exception the Johnson landslide in 1964.
7. U.S. Department of Commerce, Bureau of the Census, and U.S. De-

The even more massive migration of the White urban population of the North to the suburbs surrounding the central cities grew in size somewhat later, shortly after World War II. In the twenty years from 1950 to 1970, the central city population of the nation increased by only 9.2 million from a base of 53.4 million—the increases coming predominantly from Southern Blacks. At the same time 35 million moved from the city to the suburbs (including Catholics and many working-class people), with Whites constituting all but 1.5 million of the migration. The events of the single decade from 1960 to 1970 show the changes even more dramatically: in Northern cities of over 100,000 population, the White population actually declined in absolute numbers, in spite of the growth of the total population and the continued decline of rural and farm population.[8]

These two great migratory waves have had, as one would expect, a major impact on social and political relationships in the major metropolitan centers of the North. The cities have grown increasingly Black, and urban social and political conflict has increasingly centered on racial struggles between traditional Democrats. The suburbs, on the other hand, having absorbed only a small percentage of the Black migration (less than 5%), have remained overwhelmingly White, still relatively free of the racial conflicts of the cities (though minority penetration of the near suburbs has begun in some areas), and much more stable and affluent than the metropolitan core cities.

Whether as a response to urban experiences, or as a result simply of a new life-style in the suburbs, or both, the suburban

---

partment of Labor, Bureau of Labor Statistics, *The Social and Economic Status of Negroes in the United States, 1970,* No. 38, p. 12. Data of the post-1970 period indicate that this influx has ended, at least temporarily; there may even be a small net migration in the opposite direction.

8. U.S. Department of Commerce, Bureau of the Census, *General Demographic Trends for Metropolitan Areas, 1960 to 1970,* Final Report, p. 12.

Democrat has been long viewed by political analysts as readily convertible to Republicanism in suburbia. Just as urbanization contributed to the shaping of new kinds of Democrats and Republicans, some social scientists have seen the economic and social changes brought about by the suburbanization of White America as weakening the political loyalty of former city Democrats.[9] A home of one's own, land, real estate taxes, new economic interests, and new social patterns revolving around family and local community were seen as somehow weakening former Democratic loyalties to a party whose interests were directed toward urban, not suburban, concerns. Through just such changes, the Democratic coalition was pictured even by recent analysts such as Kevin Phillips as giving way to a new emerging Republican majority, a majority built in large part upon the political aftermath in the North of both of these mass migrations: Black migration that has racially politicized the Northern cities, and White suburban migration that has threatened the loyalty of traditional Democrats, particularly Catholics.[10]

Much of the critical analysis in the following chapters is therefore directed toward gaining a clearer view of just what changes have actually occurred in the urban "core" of the Democratic coalition in these critical regions, why these changes have occurred, and how these changes are shaping the future of Democratic politics. It would be hard to imagine that such massive movement of population together with attendant changes in the socioeconomic environment since World War II would not have had some important political effects upon the behavior of former urban Democrats. But what is the actual nature of the change and its meaning politically? Complex political changes have indeed occurred, but, as we shall see, not the kinds of changes that have been heretofore predicted.

9. See William H. Whyte, Jr., *The Organization Man* (New York: Simon & Schuster, 1956), for the first major statement of political conversion.
10. Kevin Phillips, *The Emerging Republican Majority* (Garden City: Doubleday, 1969), pp. 175–80.

THE SUBURBS AND DEMOCRATIC LOYALTY

While the suburban style of living was available in the 1920s, it was a community form that was economically feasible only for a select few. Not until the dramatic acceleration of suburbanization after World War II was the movement to become one of mass proportions, propelled by the explosive economic and social dynamics that followed the war. Governmental incentives to ease a critical housing shortage, prosperity, new low-cost methods of building, and other social and psychological dynamics combined to unleash the energy and resources for the large-scale suburbanization that followed.

Social scientists as well as popular commentators have long found this new mass phenomenon to be worthy of both ridicule and praise, as well as a stimulus for some important analytical work. Various social scientists have, in fact, uncovered unique new social patterns developing in suburbia, patterns that resulted from the possibilities of new land development, as well as from the personal motivations of the population.[11]

It would seem reasonable for these new patterns of life, developing within a new and different population mix, to be reflected in the social and political relationships in the local community—and research has clearly shown this to be the case.[12] But while

11. Wendell Bell, "Familism and Suburbanization," and Sylvia Fleis Fava, "Contrasts in Neighboring," in William M. Dobriner, ed., *The Suburban Community* (New York: G. P. Putnam's Sons, 1958). See also William M. Dobriner, *Class in Suburbia* (Englewood Cliffs, N.J.: Prentice-Hall, 1963).

12. See, for example, Robert C. Wood, *Suburbia: Its People and Their Politics* (Boston: Houghton Mifflin, 1958); Charles E. Gilbert, *Governing the Suburbs* (Bloomington and London: Indiana University Press, 1967); Herbert J. Gans, *The Levittowners–Ways of Life and Politics in a New Suburban Community* (New York: Pantheon, 1967); and Bennett M. Berger, *Working-Class Suburb: A Study of Auto Workers in Suburbia* (Berkeley and Los Angeles: University of California Press, 1969).

social scientists have significantly enriched our understanding of the *local* political response to suburban problems, very little major research has linked these new social and psychological patterns to changes in *national politics;* that is, to changes in the overall *presidential* voting patterns of the suburbs. If the suburban way of life changes or weakens Democratic Party loyalty by some subtle mechanisms, and if suburbanization remains the trend of the future, will the old Democratic coalition continue to shrink?

Attempts to measure loosening Democratic loyalty by analysis of quantitative data have added a series of valuable studies to the literature of suburbanization, but with conflicting overall results—some finding evidence favoring a swing to the Republicans, some finding a Democratic advantage in suburbanization, and some, like Frederick Wirt et al., seeing little defection of any kind.[13] But in any case quantitative analyses have already provided enough conflicting evidence for us to doubt the validity of the belief in the massiveness of suburban conversion so popular in the 1950s and 1960s.

The overgeneralizations about the extent of suburban conversion to Republicanism will be seen to be rooted in three broad misconceptions. First, the susceptibility of urban migrants to the conforming pressures of suburban middle-class life was overstated. Second, many suburbs were working class, not middle class, from their beginnings, and, consequently, there were no middle-class pressures. Third, and most important, was the mistaken assumption that the relationship of party to socio-economic status would continue to be as it was in the 1930s, with a very marked preference of the middle class for the Republican Party. This was simply not the case. The Democratic coalition was not locked into a strictly working-class constituency, but rather was able to recruit large numbers of the new middle class, many of them suburban.[14]

13. Frederick M. Wirt, Benjamin Walter, Francine Rabinowitz, Deborah Hensler, *On the City's Rim: Politics and Policy in Suburbia* (Lexington, Mass.: D. C. Heath, 1972), pp. 61–80. For a summary of other suburban voting studies see Appendix B, Note 4.
14. Everett Ladd, for example, showed graphically that as the middle class

But serious questions still remain. Are there still causative elements in suburban life which, though incapable of bringing about a massive conversion, exert steady and significant pressures that weaken former Democratic ties? Two specific questions must be answered. First, does affiliation with a political party actually change after a move to the suburbs, a change that can be attributed to suburbanization itself? And second, do those suburbanites who identify with the Democratic Party vote with the same degree of loyalty for Democratic presidential candidates as do the Democrats of the city; or has suburban life changed their behavior while leaving their political self-conceptions untouched? Therefore, it is especially instructive for our purposes to inquire into the specific presidential voting patterns of the major metropolitan centers of the East and Midwest, the essential cornerstones of the national Democratic vote.[15]

TRANSPLANTATION OR CONVERSION

Our first test of whether any particular conversion theory of suburban politics is a close approximation of reality comes from a test of the changeability of political affiliation after residence in the suburbs. The stories that abound indicating that new Democratic suburbanites change their registration (1) in order to vote in the only meaningful primaries (Republican), because Democrats rarely win general elections; or (2) in order to "fit in" with the community and be like the others; or (3) because of a real change in po-

---

expanded after World War II, it identified increasingly with the Democratic Party. See Everett Carll Ladd, Jr., *American Political Parties: Social Change and Political Response* (New York: W. W. Norton, 1970), p. 284.

15. What are essentially the core urban groups, Catholics and labor unionists, are housed predominantly in these two regions. In addition, the urban and suburban distinction in the sprawling cities of the West lacks the analytical validity that it has for the older, densely populated and industrialized metropolitan areas of the East and Midwest and is therefore less meaningful.

TABLE 1.   Change in Party Registration Among Residents in Midwestern and Eastern Suburbs[a] According to Length of Time in Community

	Midwest				East			
Length of Time in Community:	*All Residents*	*Life-long Residents*	*Over 10 Yrs.*	*10 Yrs. or Less*	*All Residents*	*Life-long Residents*	*Over 10 Yrs.*	*10 Yrs. or Less*
(Sample Sizes)	(296)	(58)	(115)	(123)	(341)	(67)	(119)	(155)
Have Changed Registration	*6%*	*7%*	*6%*	*6%*	*10%*	*7%*	*15%*	*8%*
Formerly Democrat	3	2	5	1	6	4	9	4
Formerly Republican	2	5	–	3	3	3	5	3
Formerly Independent	1	–	1	2	1	–	1	1

Source: Reformulation of Harris Suburban Survey, 1971
   [a] Suburbs included are those around cities of over 150,000 population.

litical values and party allegiance, are not borne out by the data. Changes in registration, as Table 1 shows, are modest, with only 10 percent of all Eastern suburbanites and 6 percent of all Midwestern suburbanites ever having changed their affiliation during their lifetime.[16]

16.   The original survey data of Louis Harris (Suburban Survey) were reformulated to isolate those suburbs around central cities of 150,000 rather than 50,000. The author's regional reformulation of Harris's survey essentially splits the densely populated "urban belt" into Eastern and Midwestern sub-regions. The East consists principally of large metropolitan areas in New York, Massachusetts, Connecticut, Rhode

We may conclude that the data offer no significant evidence that suburban life-style, per se, brings substantial changes in affiliations. The data also indicate that switches in registration, when they do occur, are *not* all in one direction, e.g., from Democratic to Republican. When the net change in registration is computed, the Democratic loss is extremely small (a Democratic loss of 1% in the Midwest and 3% in the East).

Two further questions come quickly to mind. First, if little conversion occurs in suburban party affiliation, how do we account for heavily Democratic cities spawning Republican suburbs? The second question, the answer to which is often taken for granted, is whether the suburbs are in reality predominantly Republican. To answer the second, more general question first, Table 2 shows that suburbs are quite unlike when we compare Midwestern and Eastern regions, even when the different regions have in common the features of being highly urbanized, industrially advanced, and built around large and long-settled cities in the urban belt.

Table 2 indicates that the political affiliation in Eastern suburbs is, in fact, heavily Republican, but in sharp contrast to the predominantly *Democratic* affiliation of the suburban Midwest. The data, independently verified by other Harris surveys, suggest that strong Republicanism, indeed a reality in the East, cannot be generalized to other regions of the country.[17]

The answer to the other question—why suburbs are heavily Republican (at least in the East) when the urban population cores from which they draw are Democratic—may be seen by examining the Eastern suburban residents and the nature of their political affiliation *when they migrated to the suburbs*. Inasmuch as it has already been demonstrated that the overall change in registration is

---

Island, Pennsylvania, and New Jersey; the Midwest encompasses Michigan, Ohio, Indiana, Wisconsin, and Illinois. See Appendix B, Note 1, for further discussion on definitions of surburbs and regions.

17. Independent verification of group and regional responses in the Harris Suburban Survey was made through comparison with other surveys, particularly the suburban segment of the Harris Urban-Suburban Survey. See Appendix B, Note 2.

TABLE 2.   Party Registration of Lifelong and Migrant Residents of Midwestern and Eastern Suburbs

	Midwest			*East*		
Length of Time in Community:	*Lifelong Residents*	*Moved from Non-Urban Area*	*Moved from Urban Area*	*Lifelong Residents*	*Moved from Non-Urban Area*	*Moved from Urban Area*
Sizes) (Sample	(43)	(69)	(91)	(49)	(71)	(97)
Registration						
Democrat	45%	49%	51%	37%	43%	39%
Republican	32	36	34	59	43	47
Independent	23	15	15	4	14	14

Source: Harris Suburban Survey[a]
[a] Sample excludes Jews and Blacks.

very small, the political affiliation of those who have migrated offers a reasonably close approximation of what the migrants' political affiliation was *before* they moved to the suburbs. The data show that the in-migration to the suburbs from strongly Democratic cities has not, contrary to popular belief, been predominantly Democratic at all, but Republican (47% Republican to 39% Democratic), and indicate a disproportionate number of Republicans among those leaving the city.

In the Eastern suburbs, the Republican majority among lifelong residents (59% Republican, 37% Democratic) receives net additions of urban Republicans, rather than masses of urban Democrats who subsequently become Republicans. What has occurred, then, is a kind of *self-selection;* those who moved to the Eastern suburbs were more likely to be Republican in affiliation *before* they moved. In other words, a disproportionate number of urban

Republicans, relative to the number of urban Democrats, have left the city for a new residence in the suburbs.

This pattern of migration in the East is in sharp contrast to the patterns that hold in the Midwest. We can see from analysis of Table 2 that lifelong residents of Midwest suburbs are predominantly Democratic and that the additions to the suburban political culture come from urban and non-urban migrants with Democratic rather than Republican roots. This analysis of the political affiliation of the vast in-migrations to suburbia suggests an important finding: *regional* influences outside the South still play a vital and perhaps underestimated role in determining overall patterns of political behavior. Later chapters will deal more fully with the social and political foundations of these differences in suburban political affiliation, but here it suffices to note the dangers of over-generalizing conclusions without proper assessment of the regional limitations.

PARTY AFFILIATION AND PARTY VOTING

The relationship between party affiliation and actual voting behavior offers a particularly interesting insight into the nature and degree of defection within the Democratic coalition.[18] Judging whether the suburban Democrat is a less loyal Democrat than his urban counterpart is important in assessing the weakening of Democratic ties through the process of suburbanization. If the suburban Democrat votes for the Democratic presidential candidate with the same relative loyalty as the urban Democrat, in spite of the less Democratic milieu in the suburbs, then suburbanization, as such, cannot bear the principal responsibility for any hypothesized weakening of Democratic loyalty.

Table 3 identifies several interesting findings when party

18. Both registration and self-identification are used in determining party affiliation, but they are used separately and not interchangeably. See Appendix A, Table 18, for a comparison of these two methods.

TABLE 3. 1968 and 1972 Presidential Vote[a] of Democrats and Independents in Midwestern and Eastern Suburbs and Cities

| | *Midwest* | | | | *East* | | | |
| | *Suburbs* | | *Cities* | | *Suburbs* | | *Cities* | |
	1968	1972	1968	1972	1968	1972	1968	1972
Democrat[b] *Voters*	(87)	(58)	(88)	(45)	(128)	(108)	(95)	(72)
Humphrey/ McGovern	77%	59%	80%	58%	67%	65%	72%	70%
Nixon	16	39	17	40	28	32	25	29
Wallace/ Other	7	2	3	2	5	3	3	1
Independent Voters	(77)	(53)	(36)	(31)	(63)	(74)	(38)	(30)
Humphrey/ McGovern	35%	22%	38%	29%	48%	21%	58%	50%
Nixon	57	78	36	71	44	76	40	50
Wallace/ Other	8	–	26	–	8	3	2	–

Source: Reformulation of Harris Urban-Suburban data[c]
   [a] Sample consists of White population only.
   [b] Affiliation determined by self-identification.
   [c] See Appendix B, Note 3, for the methodological techniques used in modifying Harris Urban-Suburban data.

identification and actual voting behavior are related to each other. First, among Democrats alone, the suburban Democrat is found to be just as loyal to his party as his urban counterpart in both 1968 and 1972. The data show that even in the strongly Republican Eastern suburbs, where Democrats are in a clear minority position, they did not switch to the Republican candidate to any greater extent than their urban counterparts. As Table 3 shows, the major increase in votes for the Republican candidate in 1972 came from Independents, who gave large majorities to Richard Nixon in the suburbs and a smaller but still substantial majority in the cities of the two regions.[19] The losses in the 1972 coalition appear to stem principally from large-scale shifts of Independents to the Republican candidate overall, and to a lesser extent from the shrinking loyalty of Democrats *in general.*

This sameness in the degree of loyalty between urban and suburban Democrats reinforces the notion that there is nothing in suburban life by itself that consistently weakens overall Democratic loyalty to the Democratic presidential candidate. While certain components of the Democratic coalition, such as Catholics or unionists, may vary in their voting loyalty depending on urban or suburban residence, the overall impact on party loyalty that can be attributed to the suburbs as such is negligible, if it exists at all.

Although it has been found that suburban Democrats overall are no less loyal to the national ticket than their urban counterparts, there remains the possibility that the suburban pattern might, in fact, be masking a defection by Democrats who moved to the suburbs from the cities. It is possible that former urban Democrats are actually less loyal but that their defections are offset by the greater loyalty of Democrats who came from small towns and other suburbs. By careful scrutiny of suburban voting behavior based upon the origin of the suburbanite, we can see that this is not the case either. Table 4 shows that the degree of loyalty (Humphrey vote among registered Democrats) among suburban Democrats who came from the cities is at least as high as it is among suburbanites who migrated from small towns and other suburbs.

As we look at those suburban Democrats who voted for Nixon (Jewish suburban voters, eliminated in Tables 2 and 4, are only 3 percent of the population in the combined regions) we find that the largest defection stems from those Eastern Democrats who do not have firm city roots (40% Nixon among former non-urban

19.   The Republican crossover vote to the Democratic candidates was small in both cities and suburbs and was not included.

TABLE 4.   1968 Presidential Vote Among Lifelong and Migrant Residents of Midwestern and Eastern Suburbs Who Are Registered Democrats

	Midwest			East		
Previous Residence:	*Lifelong Residents*	*Moved from Non-Urban Area*	*Moved from Urban Area*	*Lifelong Residents*	*Moved from Non-Urban Area*	*Moved from Urban Area*
(Sample Sizes)	(19)	(34)	(47)	(18)	(30)	(38)
Registered Democrats who:						
Voted Humphrey	68%	68%	64%	61%	50%	66%
Voted Nixon	26	15	28	11	40	21
Voted Wallace	–	3	4	–	–	5
No Vote	5	14	4	28	10	8

Source: Harris Suburban Survey[a]
   [a] Sample excludes Jews and Blacks

Democrats vs. 21% among former urban Democrats). Though the samples are small, the evidence points to the fact that the city Democrat, who has changed his life-style in the suburbs, is at least as loyal as the non-city Democrat, and probably more so.

Before turning to some of the key groups for examination, we should be warned about the risks involved in long-term projections of population dynamics based on current trends. We have seen from the data an interesting self-selection in the migration from Eastern cities, a pattern not seen in the Midwest, and one that demonstrates that internal metropolitan migration patterns have important regional variations. But just as the data reflect regional differ-

TABLE 5. Party Registration of Midwestern and Eastern Suburban Residents According to Length of Time in Community

| Length of Time in Community: | Midwest | | | East | | |
	Lifelong Resi-dents	Over 10 Years	10 Years or Less	Lifelong Resi-dents	Over 10 Years	10 Years or Less
(Sample Sizes)	(43)	(87)	(72)	(49)	(90)	(78)
Registration:						
Democrat	45%	49%	53%	37%	30%	54%
Republican	32	39	29	59	59	30
Independent	23	12	18	4	11	16

Source: Harris Suburban Survey[a]
[a] Sample excludes Jews and Blacks

ences, they also show some changes over time. Table 5 shows just
how dangerous it is to assume that the trends of the past will continue unchanged; it also indicates how gross numbers can often obscure new and important demographic changes that cannot be
observed without careful attention to time intervals.[20]

Table 5 shows that in the East the more recent suburban migrants (i.e., residents of less than 10 years' standing) are dis-
tinctly unlike their fellow suburbanites as far as political affiliation
is concerned. Looking at lifelong residents of the suburbs in the
East and at those who have lived in the suburbs for more than 10
years, we note a similar pattern of political affiliation, strongly Republican in both cases, and in roughly the same proportion (lifelong residents, 59% Republican, 37% Democratic; 10-year-plus
residents, 59% Republican, 30% Democratic). When we look at

20. Longitudinal data would be the most helpful, of course, but such data
are not available. However, some values of time can be derived from
cross-sectional data.

more recent suburbanites, those who have lived fewer than 10 years in the suburbs, we see a pattern that is very different (54% Democratic, 30% Republican). The fact that these migrants may be younger than those who have lived for more than 10 years in a suburb can by no means explain this large change in affiliation; we have already demonstrated that registration changes very modestly over time (see Table 1).

What this elaboration of the data shows is the probability of a much more generalized pattern of Eastern metropolitan migration in the past 10 years compared with the earlier self-selective Republican migrations. It would appear that the migrations up to 1960 attracted primarily individuals with prior Republican political affiliation; these were probably more upper-middle-class than those who have moved to the suburbs more recently, and their political orientation was different. It is probable that the "self-selection" wave of suburban migration in the East has ended, and there is the likelihood that the new Democratic wave will gradually produce greater Democratic gains in a heretofore Republican stronghold.

The evidence introduced in this chapter demonstrates that no continuous wholesale defections are taking place in the suburbs toward Republicanism, and that whatever looseness exists in suburban party loyalty is present at least to the same extent in the cities—though not necessarily for the same reason. But the fact that no generalized defections are taking place due to the dispersal of the urban population does not necessarily mean that suburbanization has not had any effect on specific components of the historic urban coalition—most particularly on Catholic and organized labor's political support. These powerful contributors to the Democratic electorate have traditionally provided the key building blocks for the Democratic urban majorities critical to presidential successes—support which has weakened in the past two decades in both scope and consistency. Their reactions pose several important questions. What are the factors involved in the weakening of these historically urban and Democratic support groups in the post World War II period? To what extent has suburbanization made any specific impact on the political loyalty of these key groups? To what degree has Black migration to the urban belt of the North affected traditional group-party relationships? And, finally, how have the parties themselves responded to the rapid shifting of group support in the mass electorate in their own efforts to build winning coalitions? To these and other questions our analysis addresses itself.

2

The Catholic Factor

The disproportionately high affiliation of Catholics with the Demo-cratic Party, and the correspondingly high White Anglo-Saxon Protestant support for the Republican Party, particularly outside the South, have frequently been noted.[1] This long association of Catholics with the Democratic Party can be traced, as will be seen, to two particularly important factors: the urban character of early Catholic immigration, and the intolerant nativist reaction of the culturally dominant, primarily Republican, White Anglo-Saxon Protestants.

Religion actually reached its most patent and intense level of expression as a national political issue in the aftermath of the 1928 nomination of Democrat Al Smith (a Catholic), after which major changes occurred in earlier, strongly sectional, voting alignments. It would be a mistake, however, to assume that the reaction to anti-Catholic outbursts which followed Smith's nomination was the principal cause that drew Catholics to the Democratic Party. The nomination of a Catholic in 1928 was more a concrete manifesta-

1. See, for example, Angus Campbell, Philip E. Converse, Warren E. Miller, and Donald E. Stokes, *The American Voter* (New York: John Wiley, 1960), pp. 301–6.

tion of Catholic strength already established within the Democratic Party than it was a reason for Catholics to become Democrats. Smith's nomination only hardened and accentuated Catholic support for the Democratic Party.

The origins of Catholic support for the Democratic Party lay chiefly in the circumstances of the early Irish migration to the United States. Unlike the large-scale, politically motivated immigration of Catholic and Protestant Germans following the abortive revolution of 1848, the Irish immigration resulted from severe, long-term economic destitution. The great famines of the 1840s and 50s had brought large-scale starvation to Ireland, and almost two million desperate natives sought relief in America between 1840 and 1859.[2]

Edward M. Levine has traced this initial major Catholic immigration to America in great detail and found that the combination of urban working-class poverty and religious prejudice was particularly important in forming political cleavages between the impoverished Catholic newcomers and the more prosperous established Protestants. He concluded that the political link between poor Catholic immigrants and the Democratic Party in Northern cities was only a natural reaction to the already existing close ties of "better class" Protestants with the Republican Party.[3]

The literature on the early urban political machines attests to the organizational and political abilities of these early Irish Catholic immigrants, who quickly established themselves in the leadership of the Democratic Party in the major Northern cities. Even long after other waves of immigration had made the Irish subordinate in number to other ethnic groups in the big cities, the Irish were still able to maintain Democratic Party leadership, largely by their skill and ability in adding important new immigrant groups to their following. The political literature of the period depicts with

2. U.S. Department of Commerce, Bureau of the Census, *Historical Statistics of the United States, Colonial Times to 1957*, II, pp. 56–59.
3. Edward M. Levine, *The Irish and Irish Politicians,* (Notre Dame: University of Notre Dame Press, 1966), p. 107.

both humor and cynicism the various techniques used by the Irish Democratic machines to cater to more recent immigrants, gaining the valuable political support of these new groups of Americans through their rudimentary (and questionable) "welfare" services.[4]

While the stronger association was between urban Catholics and local Democratic politics, the social legislation of the Roosevelt administration during and after the Depression of the 1930s broadened and fostered Catholic loyalty to the national party. The welfare programs of the 1930s and the Federal government's encouragement of labor union organizations through the passage of the Wagner Act in 1935 further strengthened the relationship between the urban working-class Catholic (who was a major beneficiary of the legislation) and his national government. By 1936 the national party as well as the local party was seen as committed to the interests of urban Catholic America.

The strength of Catholic support for the national party, however, has not remained constant over the years, and since the election of Harry Truman in 1948, when over two out of three Catholic voters supported the Democratic candidate, Catholic support for the national Democratic ticket has weakened considerably. Survey research has shown that the Catholic vote for the Democratic presidential candidate fell to lows of 57 percent and 53 percent in 1952 and 1956, respectively, before rising dramatically to 82 percent for the Catholic nominee, John F. Kennedy, in 1960. Catholic loyalty to the Democratic candidate slipped slightly, to 75 percent, in 1964, then further to 61 percent in 1968 during the three-party race involving Nixon, Humphrey, and Wallace, and finally to 43 percent in 1972 in the contest between Nixon and McGovern.[5]

4. Harold F. Gosnell, *Machine Politics: Chicago Model* (2nd ed., Chicago: University of Chicago Press, 1968), pp. 70–81; Finley Peter Dunne, *Mr. Dooley's Opinions* (New York, 1901).
5. Robert Axelrod, "Where the Vote Comes From: An Analysis of Electoral Coalitions, 1952–1968," *American Political Science Review*, LXVI, (March 1972), 11–20, for 1952–68 data; for 1972 data see Communications, *APSR*, LXVIII, (June 1974), 717–20.

This change in the consistency and amount of Catholic support for the Democratic presidential candidate has been attributed to a number of factors: the decrease in anti-Catholic prejudice and the consequent decline in the religious cleavage of party politics; the rise of Catholics from a predominantly working-class status to equal status with the Protestants in socio-economic terms; and, finally, the increasing numbers of Catholics being raised in a middle-class, suburban life-style. And the data clearly show both that Catholics have become, along with other Americans, more suburban than urban, and that their socio-economic status equals that of Protestants.[6]

If city life, working class roots, and religious prejudice were the principal sources of the Catholic affiliation with the Democratic Party, what happens to this affiliation when Catholics become heavily middle-class, largely suburban, and relatively unaffected by anti-Catholic prejudice? Kevin Phillips has answered this question by predicting an "emerging Republican majority," one based largely on the evaporation of the disproportionate Democratic support among Catholics, who, while only 26 percent of the population, have provided an average of almost 40 percent of the Democratic vote from 1952 to 1972.[7] To deepen our understanding of the Catholic factor in American politics, we turn our attention next to an analysis of the interaction of religious association, suburban life-style, and voting, and consequently to the role of religion in presidential party politics.

CATHOLICS IN CITIES AND SUBURBS

When the survey research data are examined, it is apparent that Catholic-Protestant differences in political behavior still remain. Table 6 shows the relationship of religion and party identification in the cities and suburbs of the Midwest and East, and demon-

6. See Appendix A, Table 19.
7. Axelrod, "Where the Vote Comes From."

TABLE 6.   Party Identification of Catholics and Protestants in Midwestern and Eastern Suburbs and Cities[a]

| Consider self: | Midwest | | | | East | | | |
	Dem.	Rep.	Ind.	(Sample Sizes)	Dem.	Rep.	Ind.	(Sample Sizes)
Catholics								
Suburbs	43%	13	36	(126)	43%	25	25	(247)
Cities	57%	12	25	(102)	59%	10	22	(133)
Protestants								
Suburbs	30%	35	29	(178)	30%	50	16	(146)
Cities	37%	28	32	(130)	35%	33	22	(49)

Source: Louis Harris, Urban-Suburban Data[b]
  [a] Party identification in 1970.
  [b] Sample includes White population only.

strates the continuing disproportionate affiliation of Catholics with the Democratic Party.

In both urban and suburban communities, and in both regions under study, Catholics identify with the Democratic Party far more frequently than do their Protestant counterparts. While *urban* Catholics, both in the East and in the Midwest, are the most Democratic, even *suburban* Catholics are much more likely to identify themselves as Democrats than as Republicans or Independents. In comparison, Protestants, overall, continue to consider themselves Republicans in these metropolitan centers under study, especially in the suburbs. While urban Protestants show a very faint plurality for the Democrats, they are clearly less Democratic than their urban Catholic counterparts.

In addition, we find significant differences in political affiliation *between* Catholics in different regions and in different types of residential communities. First, clear regional differences appear when Catholic political affiliation in the Midwestern and Eastern suburbs is studied. Suburban Catholics are more likely to be Republican in the East than in the Midwest. Second, among Eastern Catholics, suburbanites are more likely to identify with the Republican Party than their urban counterparts.[8]

These findings are in harmony with the analysis in the preceding chapter which showed a much stronger Republican affiliation in Eastern suburbs in general, and that general finding is reflected specifically in the greater Republican affiliation of Catholics as well. However, it is important to note again that the spread, or gap, between Catholic political affiliation in the Eastern cities and suburbs cannot be viewed simply as the result of suburban political conversion, for clearly if suburbanization were a consistently determining political factor, then suburban political behavior in the Midwest should show an urban/suburban differential similar to that in the East. The fact that it does not indicates that factors other than suburbanization are involved in the increased Republicanism of Eastern Catholics.

Even when we consider actual voting behavior rather than political affiliation, we see that suburban residence by itself does not decrease political loyalty among Catholic Democrats.

Although Catholic Democratic defections were not small in 1968 and 1972 (but then again neither were defections of any Democrats), the extent of political defection among Catholic Democrats was not related to suburban or urban residence in either geographic region. Table 7 shows conclusively that the type of residential community, urban or suburban, does not account for increased voting defections among Catholics, because urban Catholic Democrats are, in fact, no more loyal to their party than are suburban Catholic Democrats.

As we attempt to account for the greater numbers of long-term Republicans among Eastern suburban Catholics than among

8.   Findings are significant at .05 and .01 levels respectively.

TABLE 7.   1968 and 1972 Presidential Vote of Democratic Catholics[a] in Midwestern and Eastern Suburbs and Cities

| Election Year: | Midwest | | | | East | | | |
| | Suburbs | | Cities | | Suburbs | | Cities | |
	1968	1972	1968	1972	1968	1972	1968	1972
(Sample Sizes)	(44)	(39)	(39)	(29)	(82)	(76)	(58)	(55)
Humphrey/ McGovern	77%	59%	75%	62%	65%	72%	64%	67%
Nixon	18	41	21	38	29	28	30	33
Wallace/ Other	5	*	4	*	6	*	6	*

* Less than 1%
Source: Harris Urban-Suburban Surveys[b]
   [a] Self-identified Democratic Catholics.
   [b] Sample includes White population only.

Catholics in the Midwest, the role of socio-economic status in suburban political culture is the first explanation that comes to mind. Earlier we noted much stronger Republican Party support in Eastern suburbs than in Midwestern suburbs, a finding that could possibly be accounted for on the basis of higher levels of socio-economic status (SES) in the Eastern suburbs than in the Midwestern. The greater affluence of the Eastern suburbs, compared with, say, the lower-SES suburbs of the Midwest, might satisfactorily explain the greater Republicanism in Eastern suburbs, if we keep in mind the association between affluence and Republicanism.

Table 8 identifies specific relationships among party, religion, and socio-economic status, and demonstrates the very complex relationship between social characteristics and political behavior.

Table 8 shows that higher SES is associated with an increasing

TABLE 8.   Party Registration in Midwestern and Eastern Suburbs as a Joint Function of Socio-economic Status[a] and Religion

	Midwest				*East*			
	Dem.	*Rep.*	*Ind.*	*(Sample Sizes)*	*Dem.*	*Rep.*	*Ind.*	*(Sample Sizes)*
Lower Socio-economic Status	40%	18%	9%	*(161)*	31%	35%	9%	*(140)*
Catholics	58	5	10	(60)	38	30	11	(71)
Protestants	29	26	8	(101)	25	41	6	(69)
Higher Socio-economic Status	27%	35%	16%	*(104)*	31%	38%	10%	*(120)*
Catholics	34	18	16	(44)	39	24	11	(75)
Protestants	22	47	17	(60)	18	62	9	(45)

Source: Harris Suburban Survey[b]

[a] See Appendix B, note 5, for details of SES scaling method.

[b] Sample includes White population only.

preference for the Republican Party, but *only* in the Midwest.[9] Even though the data show that the Eastern suburbs are, in fact, more affluent, with relatively more people in the higher SES group than in the Midwest, can we therefore conclude that the relative affluence of Eastern suburbs accounts for the higher degree of Republicanism in the East among Catholics—i.e., more affluence, therefore more Republicanism? The answer is clearly negative.

In the first place, high-status Catholics in the East are essentially no different from low-status Catholics in party affiliation, whereas we would expect more Republican Catholics at the higher level. In addition, when we examine lower status suburbanites in the East and Midwest, we note that Midwestern Catholics are over-

9. These findings were independently verified by a comparative analysis with suburban preferences from the Harris Urban-Suburban surveys.

whelmingly affiliated with the Democrats (58% D, 5% R, 10% I) compared to the more equal party split among the lower SES Catholics in the Eastern suburbs (38% D, 30% R, 11% I). These findings indicate that the overall differences between Midwestern and Eastern suburbs are not adequately accounted for by differences in socio-economic status.[10] The survey research data show that political cleavages among Catholics along status lines are inconclusive, forcing us to look into other factors such as specific political values and party relationships in these regions for causal relationships that might explain more fully such variations in political coalitions.

CATHOLIC POLITICAL CULTURE: PAST AND PRESENT

The evidence of political history has led to a broad consensus among scholars that American Catholics in the nineteenth century were indeed "conservative" in their approach to social and political change.[11] Powerful opposition by Catholics to the liberal "reform movement" of the nineteenth century has been demonstrated, showing that on the whole the Irish—the first Catholic group to immigrate on a large scale—were wary and suspicious of the new middle-class "reforms" which stressed personal values very different from theirs, such as temperance and the evils of smoking. The Irish responded with deep antipathy to the patronizing concern of Prot-

10. A counter-hypothesis might explain these data on the basis of the greater acculturation of Eastern ethnic Catholics compared with Midwestern ethnic Catholics, because they have "lived more generations in America." But this hypothesis is not valid. Appendix A, Table 20, shows the greater potential acculturation of the Catholic population of the *Midwest,* which has a smaller—not larger—percentage of newer immigrants, among Catholics, than the East.

11. Leonard Wibberly, *The Coming of the Green* (New York: Holt, 1958), pp. 136–40; Andrew M. Greeley, *The Catholic Experience: An Interpretation of the History of American Catholicism* (Garden City, New York: Doubleday, 1967).

estant reformers whose interest seemed, in the eyes of the early Catholic immigrants, to lie less in alleviating dismal urban poverty than in bringing Irish Catholics into conformity with Protestant standards and life-style.[12]

Again, as the reform movement turned toward the "liberal" issue of abolition, it came into conflict with the prevailing "conservative" Catholic views on slavery. First, the "uplifting" theological views of Protestants on the nature and changeability of man clashed with the more pessimistic views of Catholics.[13] Second, and more important politically, Catholics fearfully perceived the economic threat to their employment opportunities that the success of the abolitionist movement would pose for them as a group. As the Civil War drew near, Blacks came into increasing competition with Irish Catholics for jobs in many Eastern cities. In Boston, for example, the Irish were frequently called "White Niggers," a name indicating explicitly both the level of social esteem in which the Irish were held and the potential source of future job competition. To the impoverished Irish of that time, their economic salvation seemed somehow to be dependent upon the continued bondage of the Black man.

The cynicism of the Irish toward social and political change appears to have been derived primarily from two principal sources: social and political impoverishment in Ireland under the English, and the patent Protestant discrimination against Catholics in America. The early Irish immigrants viewed with scorn the pretensions of Protestant "reform," for they could not forget that while Protestant preachers spoke eloquently against slavery on moral

12. Levine, *op. cit.,* p. 93.
13. The "Catholic" view discussed here is not that of Church doctrine but rather the situation as perceived by "Catholics." The church view certainly was not *for* slavery, but it did accept it as evidence of human frailty and held that it was not *necessarily* evil. See John Tracy Ellis, *American Catholicism* (Chicago: University of Chicago Press, 1956), p. 87. For example, The *Boston Pilot* in 1839 counseled acceptance of slavery by warning its readers against helping the abolitionist cause in any way.

grounds, the newspapers and notices on local bulletin boards almost always carried the warning "No Irish Need Apply."[14] The unique confrontation of immigrant Catholic culture and Protestant American reaction had somehow, in its early stages, produced a political culture that could hardly be described as "liberal" in any sense of the term. Viewing the future with a dourness and suspicion born of his own experience, the early Catholic immigrant simply did not share the confidence of other Americans in social and political progress.

But what of the Catholic today, both participant in and product of the changing political dynamics of the last half-century? Does he still see socio-political change in such threatening terms? Although certain moral issues, such as abortion and birth control, place Catholics in a relatively conservative position (where they have much non-Catholic company), survey research data suggest that, on at least two major spectra of national political opinion, Catholics are more liberal than Protestants. Catholic political opinion, particularly on governmental activism in social and economic affairs, will be seen to have undergone a major change in the last 35 years, and while individual Catholics do, indeed, cover the full range of belief from very conservative to very liberal (as do Protestants), the data indicate that the vital center of Catholic political opinion is significantly more liberal than the center of White Protestant political opinion.

American Catholics appear to have changed fundamentally their attitudes toward the use of national governmental power, in regard both to socio-economic welfare and to racial policy. The cynicism and distrust of political and social change, and the anti-Negro feelings typical of the early Catholic immigrant, have largely been erased, so that today Catholics have greater confidence than Protestants in the desirability and effectiveness of governmental action to alleviate major social problems by political means. While

14.   George M. Potter, *To the Golden Door* (Boston: Little, Brown, 1960), pp. 374–76.

there are certain ethnic differences among Catholics that are reflected in presidential voting patterns, overall, the Catholic electorate has changed politically, showing evidence of a new synthesis of the "Catholic" and the "American" aspects of its experience; and this has markedly changed, as we shall see, the fundamental basis of the relationship between Catholics and the Democratic Party.[15] While Catholics were originally a less progressive force for social change in American politics—with only strong ethnic ties to local party organizations—their present-day preference for the Democrats will be seen to be based on the overall harmony of a more liberal Catholic electorate with the more liberal national political party, rather than on simply memories of past local linkages.

One of the difficulties in studying the liberal political values of groups and comparing them on this basis lies in the different definitions given to the very terms "liberal" and "conservative," terms whose meanings vary according to their application to such matters as social welfare activism, freedom of speech, racial issues, or international affairs. Gerhard Lenski sought to find if these different meanings of liberalism were related to each other among different sociological groups but found, as did S. M. Lipset, that the relationship was not highly consistent. For example, members of the working class scored high on social welfare liberalism measures but low on issues involving rights of free speech and internationalism.[16]

A similar multi-dimensionality to the term "liberalism" was found in a study carried out by Lloyd Free and Hadley Cantril

15. See Andrew M. Greeley, Norman Nie, and Barbara Currie, "Ethnics and the Coalition" (unpublished paper, University of Chicago, 1971), Table 4; see also Mark R. Levy and Michael S. Kramer, *The Ethnic Factor: How America's Minorities Decide Elections* (New York: Simon & Schuster, 1972), pp. 140–89.

16. Gerhard Lenski, *The Religious Factor: A Sociological Study of Religious Impact on Politics, Economics and Family Life* (rev. ed., Garden City: Doubleday, 1963), p. 210. Seymour Martin Lipset, *Political Man: The Social Bases of Politics* (Garden City: Anchor Books, 1960), pp. 87–115, 303–18.

some six years later, in 1964. The studies they conducted sought to differentiate liberals and conservatives along three different spectra of political opinion: domestic social and economic programs, international policy, and ideological concerns. After examining the results of their extensive surveys of political opinion, they found that the clearest way to differentiate liberals from conservatives in the United States was on the basis of "operational liberalism," defined by them as the relative willingness to involve the national government in the resolution of specific socio-economic problems in such fields as health, housing, employment, and poverty; i.e., programmatic liberalism.[17]

In order to understand the basis of political divisions in America more fully, Free and Cantril described along with the operational spectrum a second spectrum of political opinion, an ideological spectrum, that dealt with more abstract political ideas about government.[18] When they compared their two scales they found that the distribution of the American population was not skewed to the liberal side, as on the operational spectrum, but instead to the conservative side. Americans, their analysis showed, think in a cautious, conservative way about abstract philosophical ideas of government, but also want a relatively active, liberal government to develop specific socially oriented programs and policies.

Of central importance for our study of group politics, Free and Cantril found that the clearest distinction between political parties in the electorate at large was on "operational" issues i.e., specific program preferences, rather than on abstract "ideological" issues, for which the overlap of Democrats and Republicans was much larger. The members of the two major political parties, it

17. Lloyd A. Free and Hadley Cantril, *The Political Beliefs of Americans: A Study of Public Opinion* (New Brunswick: Rutgers University Press, 1967), p. 5.
18. The differences in content of the two spectra can be seen by comparing examples of the questions asked for agreement or disagreement: the Federal government is interfering too much in state and local matters (general and ideological); the Federal government should increase grants to build public housing (specific and operational).

was found, had far larger differences on operational programs than they had on philosophical or ideological issues.

The operational (or programmatic) differences present in the 1960s have continued to define the electorate along partisan lines in the 1970s, although general enthusiasm for initiating new large programs has diminished. Rather than developing numerous new programs, Democrats are more likely to want to maintain or expand existing programs, while Republicans on balance want to reduce them.[19] Nevertheless, specific new programs in the 1970s, such as national health insurance, have generated broad popular approval (Harris, 1974), suggesting that those new programs that are not perceived to favor disproportionately the poor and heavily Black segments of the population still have substantial support. Thus, for example, funding of education, health care, and aid to stimulate the economy still are viewed favorably by the electorate (with clear partisan divisions) despite continued lip-service to the general desire to "reduce the size of the government."[20]

One other spectrum of opinion studied by Free and Cantril deserves brief mention, primarily because of the relative insignificance of the findings. The authors developed a third spectrum of political support based on responses to international questions along an isolationist-internationalist continuum i.e., a foreign policy scale. Their results indicated that divisions along political party lines or religious lines were not at all clear indicators of international policy preferences. At best, their "international spectrum" showed only very slight divisions among partisan and religious groups.[21]

Even after the impact of the Vietnam War had been felt by

19. The Gallup Survey, *New York Times,* August 31, 1975, p. 26.
20. The popular appeal of health and education programs was undoubtedly an important factor in the successful override of the President's vetoes on the funding of these programs in 1975. On issues where benefits go disproportionately to the poor and Black; e.g., public housing subsidies, disapproval and partisan disagreement increases substantially. See the Harris Survey, *New York Post* March 19, 1973, June 10, 1974.
21. *Ibid.,* pp. 59–93.

the electorate, those identifying with the two major political parties still continued essentially the same "non-partisan" approach to foreign policy, as Richard W. Boyd found:

> As one would predict on a matter of foreign policy, there are no long-term, partisan aspects of people's attitudes about Vietnam. Republicans and Democrats are almost equally likely to endorse solutions ranging from pulling out of Vietnam entirely to taking a stronger stand even if it means invading North Vietnam.[22]

Leaving aside the complexity of short-run electoral decisions for the moment, we can see that for long-term alignments the operational spectrum (and to a lesser extent the ideological spectrum) defines a major body of political opinion in which religious and party differences are most clearly reflected. In order to add a new dimension to Free and Cantril's analysis, the data were reformulated to add another level of analysis, one that broke out divisions along the operational (programmatic) spectrum by party, religion, and region for the purpose of further examining the interaction between the political values of Democrats and Republicans, Catholics and Protestants.[23]

As can be seen by an inspection of Figure A, Catholic and Protestant party affiliations with the Democratic and Republican parties respectively are grounded in shared political values of do-

22. Richard W. Boyd, "Popular Control of Public Policy: A Normal Vote Analysis of the 1968 Election," *American Political Science Review*, LXVI, (June 1972), p. 432. Although long-term party affiliation seems unresponsive to international policies, this does not mean that short-term effects of unsuccessful foreign policy decisions may not be substantial in any single election or group of elections. Boyd identified this short-run liability by showing the significantly lower than normal vote by traditional Democratic presidential voters when their Vietnam policy preference was at variance with the perceived position of candidate Hubert Humphrey.

23. The urbanized states of the East and the Midwest were again isolated from the more rural states in a manner similar to the earlier revisions of Louis Harris's data. The data were then retabulated to unveil differences in Catholic/Protestant political opinion and Democratic/Republican political opinion in each region separately.

mestic political policy in both regions. Specifically, the evidence indicates that in both key regions under study Republicans and Protestants share conservative political values. At the other end of the spectrum, Catholics and Democrats share liberal values. While there is an overlapping of opinion among Protestants and Catholics within parties, the general configuration of values suggests, as Daniel Elazar has observed, a strong association of religious subcultural values with like partisan political values.[24]

In Figure A, the differences between regions on political values are very much in evidence. When the spectra are compared, Easterners are, in general, more liberal than Midwesterners, whether one compares party with party or religious sub-community with religious sub-community. This regional difference also holds for Independents, who fall between Republicans and Democrats in each category of opinion, tending, as one might expect, to the liberal side in the East and to the conservative side in the Midwest.

While group divisions are sharper along the operational spectrum than on other measures of liberalism, it would be inaccurate to see Catholic liberalism as solely rooted in a desire for greater scope for domestic socio-economic programs. Catholic liberalism, even on the ideological scale, is modestly, but still significantly, higher than Protestant liberalism, most clearly in the Midwest. Even though ideological liberalism appears a less explanatory measurement of political divisions, Catholics nonetheless scored relatively higher than Protestants on this measurement, which is defined by issues that were more abstract and systemic in nature.[25]

But can the closeness of Catholic values to Democratic values help answer earlier unresolved questions, such as why Catholics in the Eastern cities and suburbs tend to affiliate themselves more

24. Daniel J. Elazar, *Cities of the Prairie* (New York: Basic Books, 1970), p. 191.
25. Although the measures are not precisely comparable, these data tentatively suggest that the Catholic ideological conservatism found in Lenski's earlier research may have undergone some change in the direction of greater liberality, possibly in response to the political orientation of the first Catholic president, John F. Kennedy.

FIGURE A. Operational and Ideological Liberalism in the Midwest and East by Party Identification and Religion

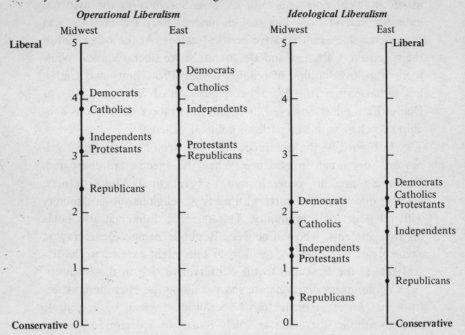

Source: Data abstract from *Political Beliefs of Americans*[a]

[a] Score is median group score.

strongly with Republicanism than those in the Midwest? Can the relatively larger defections to Republicanism among Eastern Catholics that we have found be attributed to the greater conservatism of Eastern Catholics in terms of political values? Clearly not. The larger proportion of Eastern Catholics who identify themselves as Republicans cannot be attributed to Catholic conservatism in that region, nor can any weakened loyalty of Catholic Democrats be so explained, for as we have seen in Figure A, Catholics in the East overall are more liberal, not less liberal, than their Catholic counterparts in the Midwest on both the operational and the ideological spectra.

There is one other important spectrum of political values that requires examination in terms of religious groups which might account for the weakening of the Catholic/Democratic relationships in the East—where, paradoxically, Catholics are more liberal. This spectrum, one that covers the dimension of *racial values* and policies among various groups, could, if Eastern Catholics were found to be more conservative racially than Midwestern Catholics, explain the drift of Eastern Catholics to Republicanism as a result of racial conservatism's cutting into operational liberalism. As we have already seen, a historical basis for resistance to Black progress (in contrast to Protestant racial reformism) has long existed among urban Catholics; it is therefore legitimate to ask whether traditional racial attitudes still persist—and whether they are inconsistent with the Catholic/Democratic and Protestant/Republican relationships observed along other political spectra.

Therefore, in an effort to gauge present-day racial liberalism and conservatism among major religious and political groups regionally, a comparative racial spectrum was constructed on issues covering governmental action to implement social integration, Black employment, school integration, and other issues of Black concern.[26] As can be seen by examining Figure B, the racial liberalism scale reveals little difference between Catholics and Protestants on these issues (whatever difference exists favors greater Catholic liberalism), indicating that any long-term movement away from the more racially liberal Democratic Party is not linked to specifically Catholic conservative racial values.[27]

The evidence demonstrates that Catholic attitudes on race have undergone a substantial change over time, and it shows present-day Catholics to be as liberal as Protestants, perhaps even

26. See Appendix B, Note 6, for the 1968 Survey Research Center questions used and scaling methodology. A note of caution on the measurement of racial liberalism and conservatism. These terms do not measure racism, although racism may or may not be involved in the specific response. They do, however, measure the degree of active support for Black social and political objectives.
27. This does not mean that the short-term racial conflicts which affect all religious groups cannot have a significant impact on voting behavior; they certainly can, as subsequent chapters will show.

FIGURE B.   Racial Attitudes[a] by Religion, Region, and Party Affiliation[b]

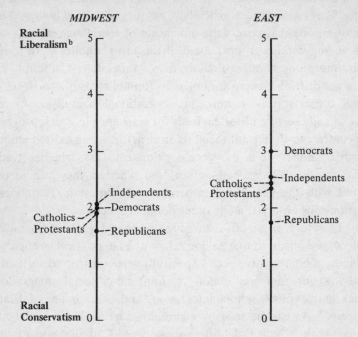

Source: Abstracted from 1968 Survey Research Center data

[a] Whites only, regions are U.S. Census Bureau definitions.

[b] Scores are group median scores on racial liberalism scale. Midwest sample sizes: Democrats (162), Republicans (121), Independents (113), Catholics (98), Protestants (338). East sample sizes: Democrats (138), Republicans (95), Independents (93), Catholics (151), Protestants (181).

more so. In addition, when consideration is given to the fact that Catholics are relatively more urban than Protestants (and consequently more often on the cutting edge of Black/White conflict at the neighborhood level), the similarity of racial liberalism scores among Protestants and Catholics is even more impressive evidence of the liberal strides by Catholics in racial matters.

Overall, the data on Catholic political behavior point to a number of important conclusions. First, Catholics have not remained predominantly Democratic primarily because of non-programmatic linkages to local party organizations (i.e., historical vestiges of tradition without political substance), but have remained so from their relatively high regard for the pursuit of liberal socio-economic welfare policies by an activist national party. In addition, their leaving their urban roots for a more affluent and different life in the suburbs has not markedly changed their affiliation with the Democratic Party, nor has suburbanization weakened the actual voting loyalty of suburban Catholic Democrats to any greater extent than it has among Democrats in general.

Taking the various spectra of political opinion together, we see that it is principally the operational spectrum that has firmly linked Catholics and Democrats along policy or "position" lines, unlike other liberalism spectra in which party ties and religious ties are more or less unrelated. While clearly not more conservative than Protestants along these other scales of opinion, Catholics are nevertheless not as closely tied to these kinds of liberalism and would, like Democrats in general, be likely to draw further away from the Democratic Party if political conflict continued primarily along racial or foreign policy divisions.

We have found that socio-economic factors, suburbanization, and differences in Catholic values cannot fully account for weakened Catholic ties to the Democratic Party that have occurred primarily in the East. As these first chapters have revealed, coalitional change among national support groups remains a complex and multifaceted process in a still vibrant federal* party system. In the chapters that follow we will examine new pieces of the puzzle that are found among the changing political relationships of other key urban Democrats in order to shed more light on the dynamics of change taking place in a fast-shifting and complex American electorate.

* The word "federal" refers to state/national relationships and when so used is not capitalized.

3

Labor and
the Democratic Coalition

The political history of the labor movement in America has been
characterized in broad terms as a transition from a non-partisan,
voluntarist, and essentially defensive approach to politics, to one
of partisanship and aggressive support for specific political policies
and candidates.[1] In tracing the development of labor participation
in the presidential coalition, it is necessary to distinguish between
two aspects of labor union politics: *labor leadership* and their executive organization on the one hand, and the mass of union members *as voters* on the other. Both these factors, singly and in their
relationship, have had important impacts on the American party
system, both within and between each of the two major political
parties.

The early AFL leadership took precautions to remain neutral
in political affairs until the opening decade of the twentieth century. However, slowly and reluctantly the early policy of non-

1. David B. Truman, *The Governmental Process: Political Interests and
Public Opinion* (New York: Knopf, 1951), pp. 66–74. Also Grant Mc-
Connell, *Private Power and American Democracy* (New York: Knopf,
1967), pp. 298–335.

partisanship among trade union leaders began to change to one of support for the Democratic Party, for by the first decade of the twentieth century, emerging anti-union pressures within the Republican Party helped bring about the formation of new political relationships.[2]

In 1906 the AFL presented a "Bill of Grievances" to President Theodore Roosevelt and the leaders of Congress, protesting the anti-labor activities of the courts and the Attorney General, and at the same time recommending legislative action to improve certain working conditions. Basically this intervention into national politics did not seek to enlist governmental aid in any positive sense; its prime objective was to free the Federation from state coercion by injunctions and anti-trust activity, thus enabling it to fight its battles with employers on a more even basis. However, even as a defensive strategy this position of the leadership initiated a new political approach between labor and the national party system. As J. David Greenstone has noted:

> The 1906 election set a pattern that, with variations from election to election, continued until at least 1922. [The AFL's] Democratic preference was not officially expressed by a formal convention resolution, but it was unmistakable nevertheless, because a Republican victory was equated with an AFL defeat.[3]

Although the increasing orientation favoring labor partisanship among the leadership was slowed by the general conservatism of the 1920s, the trade union rank and file slowly began to follow the general orientation of their leaders in their pro-Democratic leanings, and they became more firmly interlocked with the Democrats by the nomination of Al Smith in 1928. The trade unions of the AFL, having within their membership a disproportionate percentage of Catholics, moved even closer to the Democratic Party

2. Vivian Vale, *Labour in American Politics* (New York: Barnes & Noble, 1971), pp. 35–44.
3. J. David Greenstone, *Labor in American Politics* (New York: Vintage Books, 1969), p. 31.

in response to the nativist, anti-Catholic bias shown by the Republican Party in that presidential campaign. As observed earlier, the Democratic Party by this time was far more accessible to Irish Catholics, and moderately more responsive to the trade union interests, and this interrelation of ethnic and class interests had a significant impact on establishing a Democratic trade union base in the urban centers of the North.

Lubell's analysis of the 1932 and 1936 election returns firmly established the importance of this interrelationship as he identified the reluctance of the Protestant working class to move their support to the Democratic Party. The socio-religious values of Northern Protestants, traditionally loyal to the Republican Party, were found to be shaken, but not reversed politically, by the deepening Depression. He uncovered evidence that the urban Protestant workers voted, on balance, for Herbert Hoover in 1932, despite Hoover's unresponsiveness to the massive unemployment among the working class.[4]

It was only in their retrospective political judgment, after the first Roosevelt administration ended in 1936, that Protestant workers joined their Catholic fellow workers in clear support for the Democratic presidential candidate. And in doing so this victory, rather than Roosevelt's first election in 1932, revealed two important political changes: first that class issues had finally overcome socio-religious traditions among Protestant laboring people; and, second, that the Democratic Party had become clearly identified by Protestant as well as Catholic workers as the preferred vehicle for the promotion of their socio-economic interests.

The Wagner Act, passed in 1935, was perceived by labor as open encouragement by the national government to organize the major mass production industries, and this, together with numerous support programs beneficial to working-class interests—such as unemployment insurance and minimum wage laws—clearly identified the Democratic Party as sympathetic to the labor movement. What had begun as a reluctant leadership preference had become, by

4.   Lubell, *Future of American Politics,* pp. 48–52.

1936, a strong political tie between the Democratic Party and the labor electorate at large. By that time, not only trade unionists but most working-class people, union and non-union, had joined in fervent support for the New Deal coalition.

In the space of only a few years, the political force of organized labor was fueled by huge increases in membership—the result of organizing the heretofore "untouchables" of the mass production industries, such as automobile, steel, and rubber. During the years between 1933 and 1939 alone, the number of organized workers went from less than three million to over eight million; some union members were recruited as the result of efforts by industrial units in the AFL, but most (almost four million) by the newly formed Committee (later Congress) of Industrial Organizations (CIO).[5]

While doctrinal and organizational cleavages continued between the leaders of the union movement, the economic conditions and political decisions of the Roosevelt administration had made firm Democrats out of a large majority of the union members themselves. The rank and file among trade unionists preferred an even more forthright and active pro-Democratic policy than did its leadership during the 1930s. It was, after all, a leadership that waited until 1932 (after three years of economic depression) before it finally endorsed compulsory unemployment insurance—and it did so with reluctance.[6]

The AFL leadership remained extremely cautious about encouraging Federal action on labor matters, largely for fear of bestirring governmental power that might eventually be used against trade unionism. On the other hand, the leadership of the new industrial unions of the CIO took a much more aggressive political position in national politics, for it lacked the suspicion and fear of government which over the years had been so characteristic of the AFL leadership. The greater interest in national party politics by the CIO unions resulted in the founding of the Political Action

5.   Greenstone, *op. cit.*, p. 41.
6.   Philip Taft, *Organized Labor in American History* (New York: Harper & Row, 1964), p. 607.

Committee (PAC), formed in 1943 for the purpose of mobilizing members of the CIO, their families, and other workers for effective political action. The CIO even proposed a common political program with the AFL, and though the offer was considered, it was subsequently refused by the AFL Executive Council because the AFL leadership felt that their traditional non-partisan political policy prevented any joint political organization from developing.[7]

From the late 1930s until as late as 1947, the AFL maintained no permanent political department and devoted only a small percentage of its resources to political activities. However, the passage of the Taft-Hartley Act in 1947 by the 80th Congress over the veto of President Truman surprised the AFL leadership with the scope and effectiveness of the anti-labor mobilization. It was, in fact, primarily in response to this political defeat that the AFL convention recommended the establishment of the Labor, Educational and Political League (LEPL) to carry on political activities similar to those already under way in the CIO.

In the election of 1952, the AFL officially endorsed its first presidential Democratic candidate and made available official organizational as well as financial resources to the national Democratic campaign. After the merger of the AFL and CIO in 1955, the Committee on Political Education (COPE) was formed to carry on the functions of PAC and LEPL, and, unlike the case in jurisdictional quarrels, the political efforts of the newly merged labor interests were from the beginning generally cooperative and productive.[8]

When comparison is made of the political activities of the CIO and AFL before the merger in 1955, it would not be fair to describe all the unions in the CIO as active and liberal and to ascribe passivity and conservatism to all unions in the AFL. Certain unions in the AFL, such as the International Ladies Garment Workers Union and many of the unions in the printing trades, were historically both active and liberal on social welfare policy and yet

7. *Ibid.,* pp. 607–8.
8. Greenstone, *op. cit.,* p. 56.

remained in the AFL. On the other hand, certain industrial unions of the CIO, such as the United Steel Workers Union, were historically less active politically and less aggressive on matters of general welfare policy. By the 1950s, however, the leaders of all the major unions were politically active, and though some of the leaders of individual labor internationals broke with the Democratic presidential candidate in 1972, the leadership overall was nevertheless deeply involved in the electoral process itself, taking positions and offering or declining organizational support for one candidate or another.

When we examine the voting patterns of union members themselves, we find that the extent of organized workers' affinity for the Democratic presidential candidate since the New Deal has been more uneven than that of the leadership. Starting in the early 1930s, rank and file support for the Democratic Party exceeded that of the union leadership, their enthusiastic support rising to a greater extent than that of the leadership. When the rank and file clashed with a leadership position (as in CIO president John L. Lewis's opposition to Franklin Roosevelt's re-election in 1940), the union members voted their own way and then deposed Lewis as CIO president, feeling that his opposition to Roosevelt had betrayed their interests.[9]

The strong preference by unionists as a group for the Democratic presidential nominee continued through the 1944 and 1948 campaigns, even though support for Truman was less solid among a number of the better paid craft unions of the AFL—a pattern that was found to continue (with AFL unionists voting approximately 5% to 10% less Democratic than CIO unionists) up through the mid 1950s.[10] However, the high level of union support for the Democratic nominee that prevailed through 1948 (approximately three to one) was not sustained through the Eisenhower years, as union support in the presidential elections dropped to

9. Samuel Lubell, "Who Elected Roosevelt?" *Saturday Evening Post,* January 25, 1941, 23–29.
10. Campbell *et al., The American Voter,* p. 312.

59 percent Democratic in 1952, and still further to 55 percent in 1956.[11]

In 1960, the nomination of a Catholic at the top of the Democratic ticket and the absence of Eisenhower on the Republican ticket helped raise union support of the Democrats to 66 percent; and then, in 1964, Barry Goldwater's outright hostility to organized labor leadership as well as to most New Deal welfare legislation pushed the Democratic percentage among unionists to a post-World War II high of 80 percent. But the increasing volatility of the labor union vote was dramatically demonstrated only four years later when Hubert Humphrey, long identified as a friend of unionism and labor leadership, was able to win a bare 51 percent of union voters, with Richard Nixon regaining some of the normally Republican union vote and George Wallace's candidacy siphoning off an estimated 15 percent (Gallup) of the union vote. Survey research studies of union voting in the 1972 election indicated an even more drastic decline in labor support, as President Nixon gained the first Republican majority among members of organized labor in the nearly four decades that scientific election survey data have been available.[12]

SUBURBANIZATION AND LABOR POLITICS

One of the most frequent explanations for the weakening of rank and file labor support for the Democratic Party is based on the assumed importance of the emerging suburban life-style among Union membership at large. It is clear that the great economic gains made from collective bargaining efforts have, in fact, made it possible for many working-class people to share in the massive migrations from the major central cities to the adjoining suburbs.

11.   Axelrod, "Where the Vote Came From," p. 14.
12.   The Gallup Poll found only 46 percent of union families voting for Democrat George McGovern. CBS News Election Day Survey indicates a slightly higher Democratic vote.

Though not all union workers' wages are sufficiently high to afford home ownership, survey research offers a dramatic insight into the extent of suburban life-style among members of organized labor. In the East, 27 percent of the suburban population is composed of union households, and in the Midwest, 37 percent; most of these households are privately owned homes.[13]

The various implications of property ownership, both the pleasures and the financial responsibilities, have been offered as plausible, although not necessarily valid, explanations of union defection during the past two decades of suburbanization. While containing some truth, these generalizations about labor and suburbanization do not take into account the complexity and variations of the party system itself, and implicitly assume a constancy of party relationships among labor unionists in different regions of the country. A clearer understanding of union behavior requires a simultaneous examination of the interaction of socio-economic and residential factors within the party system and the regional subsystems.

Table 9 compares the political affiliations of union members and non-union members in Eastern and Midwestern suburbs, as well as their presidential voting behavior. It identifies once again the distinct regional difference between suburbs on a party basis—the Eastern suburbs being significantly more Republican than those in the Midwest.

As our earlier analysis might lead us to suspect, the strong Republicanism of Eastern suburbs overall is also reflected in the relatively high Republican registration among union members—the ratio of registered Democrats to Republicans among union members being approximately seven to five in the East compared to nearly three to one in the Midwest.

The relatively higher Republican affiliation among Eastern suburban unionists cannot be explained as the result of political conversion, since we have already seen that the extent of net party change over time is small (see Table 1). The data have shown that

13.   These data are from the Harris Suburban Survey.

TABLE 9.   Party Registration and 1968 Presidential Vote of
Union Members and Non-members in Midwestern and Eastern
Suburbs

	Midwest		East	
	Union Members	*Non-Union Members*	*Union Members*	*Non-Union Members*
(Sample Sizes)	(85)	(120)	(63)	(154)
Registration				
Democrat	60%	40%	49%	38%
Republican	21%	45%	36%	52%
Independent	19%	15%	15%	10%
(Sample Sizes)	(88)	(134)	(65)	(154)
1968 Presidential Vote				
Humphrey	60%	24%	42%	32%
Nixon	33%	73%	52%	64%
Wallace	7%	3%	6%	4%

Source: Harris Suburban Survey[a]
   [a] Sample excludes Jews and Blacks.

for the vast majority of union members, their relatively greater
Republicanism has been the result of a long-term, self-selective
migration by Republican-oriented unionists and not, in the main,
by suburb-induced political conversion. Union Republicanism appears to have strong, long-term roots in the East, and it appears
that regional party relationships, not residential community type,
are more important factors in determining the degree of Republican inroads into Democratic/labor solidity.

   The regional differences in union political behavior are even more dramatic when the 1968 presidential vote of suburban unionists is analyzed. As can be seen in Table 9, Hubert Humphrey received almost a two-to-one majority of the union vote in the Midwest, while in the East, suburban union members actually gave Richard Nixon a majority of their votes.[14] These very large regional differences in the voting behavior of organized labor should give pause to any analysis based on specific suburbs or suburbanization alone.

One could argue again that the higher socio-economic status of Eastern suburbanites could account for their greater Republicanism. But, as in the case of the earlier analysis of Catholics, SES does not sufficiently explain regional differences in the labor vote. Analysis of the data (see Appendix A, Table 21) shows that union members in the East lean more heavily toward the Republican candidates than do union members in the Midwest, and this is true at both high and low SES levels.

The evidence suggests that working-class and party relationships are under distinct regional influence, since even lower-status union members do not perceive the presidential candidates from the same point of view in terms of policy in the different regional political sub-systems.[15] As the following chapter will show, these regional relationships persisted in the 1972 election, even in the face of the landslide defeat of the Democratic candidate George McGovern.

Because of the tie between political attitudes and political partisanship, another explanation of the heavier Democratic voting in the Midwest might be that union members in the Midwest have more liberal political attitudes than union members in the East

14. These regional differences were verified independently by comparison with the data from Harris Urban-Suburban studies.
15. This regional difference among unionists is also pronounced on an occupational basis among all blue-collar workers, union and non-union. In the Eastern suburbs almost two out of three of all blue-collar workers voted for Richard Nixon, while in the Midwest a majority of blue-collar workers, union and non-union, voted for Hubert Humphrey (from Harris Suburban Survey).

and therefore the greater support for the more operationally liberal party (Democratic) could conceivably be a reflection of this general association of liberal values with Democratic partisanship. Hypothetically, then, the more densely working-class neighborhoods in the Midwest could be viewed as more effective transmitters and reinforcers of "appropriate" voting (i.e., unionists communicating to fellow union members the close association between union interests and the interests of the Democratic Party).[16]

This plausible hypothesis, however, is not valid. Figure C indicates that, contrary to the hypothesized expectations, Midwestern union members are not more liberal than Eastern unionists, but less so (i.e., *less* favorable to operationally liberal domestic political concerns as well as those more ideological in nature).

The large regional differences on the operational liberalism scale between Midwest and Eastern union members point to unique relationships between working-class values and the regional political system, suggesting that the "union factor" and the "party factor" are in a very complex interrelationship. Regional *party differences,* not just attitudinal differences, clearly appear to affect the translation of rank and file union values into political behavior.

Figure C shows the position of union members and nonmembers relative to the positions of Democrats, Republicans, and Independents on both the operational and the ideological liberalism scales. As seen in the religion/party relationship observed earlier, union members are relatively higher than non-members on both scales, and this is true both in the Midwest and the East. Figure C and the voting results in Table 9 thus point to the same puzzling phenomenon found in Chapter 2: the key groups, in this case unionists and Democrats, share similar liberal programmatic values, and yet greater defections from the Democratic ranks occur

16. See Robert E. Lane, *Political Life: Why and How People Get Involved in Politics,* (New York: Free Press, 1959), p. 262. This tie has also been made by sociologists, such as Bennett Berger in *Working Class Suburb;* the data introduced here are offered not in refutation of a sociological thesis, but rather as evidence that other intervening variables are also involved in any explanation.

FIGURE C. Operational and Ideological Liberalism in the Midwest and East by Party Identification and Union Membership

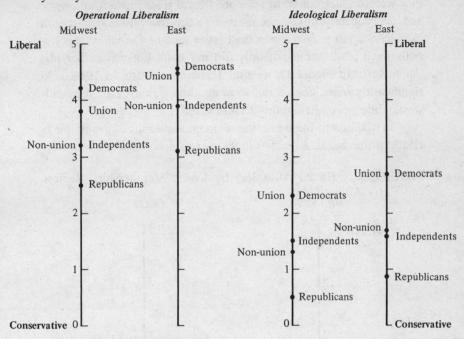

Source: Data abstract from *Political Beliefs of Americans*[a]

[a] Score is *median* score of respondents in each group. See Appendix B, note 8 for sample sizes.

among the organized laboring people in the very region (the East) where union members are more, rather than less, liberal.

As in the earlier analysis of Catholics, we cannot explain this Eastern union defection on the basis of a greater similarity in political values between rank and file Democrats and Republicans in the East, for the distance in political values between Republican and Democratic partisans is essentially the same in the two regions. Consequently, defections in the East are not more likely than they are in the Midwest because of narrower differences between rank and file partisans on socio-economic welfare liberalism.

The regional differences in labor's political behavior might be accounted for by the racial attitudes of Midwest labor unionists, if they were, in fact, found to be more liberal than Eastern unionists, and consequently linked themselves to the more liberal party on race-related issues. But, as in the earlier case of Catholics, this hypothesized relationship not only did not hold, but was rather just the reverse. In Figure D, we find Eastern unionists in 1968 held significantly *more liberal racial views* than unionists in the Midwest, while more often voting *Republican*.

In addition to the persisting regional variations of group/party relationships, another factor should also be noted: labor's relatively

FIGURE D.   Racial Attitudes[a] by Union Membership, Region, and Party Affiliation[b]

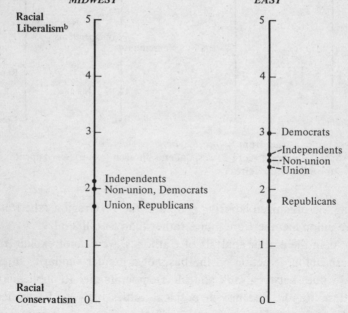

Source: Abstracted from 1968 Survey Research Center data

[a] Whites only, regions are U.S. Census Bureau definitions.

[b] Scores are median scores on racial liberalism scale. Midwest Sample Sizes: Union (112), Non-Union (293), Democrats (162), Republicans (121), Independents (113), East Sample Sizes: Union (109), Non-Union (228), Democrats (138), Republicans (95), Independents (93).

conservative racial attitudes in the Midwest are matched by the conservative views of Republicans, while Democrats score only slightly higher. This is in contrast to the values held in the East where unionists score higher than all Midwestern groups and fall midway between Democrats and Republicans.

The clustering of labor and non-labor groups as well as all partisans in the same general range in the Midwest indicates that racial views do not seem to be a significant basis for regular party cleavages in that region—with union attitudes closest, in fact, to Republican attitudes and party ties closer to the Democrats. In the East, on the other hand, labor unionists are far more liberal on racial policies than Republican rank and file, and yet tend to be relatively more Republican in their politics than Midwestern unionists.

The fact that defections from the Democratic candidate are greater among generally more liberal labor unionists and Catholics in the East points to the complexity of the electoral decision in the party system in America, where, as we shall see, not just political conflict but the *perceived salience of conflict* in the voter's mind is critical to specific electoral choices. How one perceives the political meaning of the party symbol "Democrat" or "Republican" is of necessity linked to the visible representations of each party, specifically the parties' candidates, and in the following chapters we shall see that the dynamic activities of party elites, first at the state level and then again at the national level, play a critical role in choosing these candidates, giving new meaning to the party symbol by their choices, and subsequently framing the political alternatives for the mass electorate.

The very choices provided by the parties in a federal party system and the vital role of party leaders and activists in selecting the party's candidate constitute a process that sharply limits and defines the actual range of choices available to the electorate, shapes the specific agendas of party conflict, and in consequence leads to new alignments of key voters in the mass coalition by restructuring the basis of party loyalty. In the chapters that follow

we will isolate and analyze some of these important *party factors*
that have led to substantial defections among key Democratic
groups in the electorate, and thereby deepen our understanding of
the linkage between party leadership, mass responses and overall
political change.

4

National Coalitions and
Federal Linkages

In seeking a fuller understanding of the factors involved in changing coalitions in American electoral politics, the analysis of party affiliation and voting loyalty of key Democrats has repeatedly pointed to significant regional variations in the political response of these groups. The fact that these groups manifest persistent regional variations even when the two regions examined share such similar characteristics of being Northern, industrially developed, and urban in character, suggests that while coalitional groups may be conceptualized and described in national terms, they still respond in the context of a *federal* political environment. For even where issues are normally considered national in character, the response to them is still significantly affected not only by socio-economic and cultural divisions but also by the nature of federal party cleavages that can sharply alter the perceived priority and the intensity of conflict and consequently the voter's response.

An examination of group voting behavior in Table 10 objectively establishes the impact of regional influence on both socio-economic groups and partisan groups. Looking at the voting behavior of a large sample of rank and file voters in the East and in

TABLE 10.   1972 Presidential Vote[a] by Region, Party, Religion, and Union Membership

	Midwest		East	
	% That Voted Nixon	*% That Voted McGovern*	*% That Voted Nixon*	*% That Voted McGovern*
	58	*42*	*56*	*44*
Democrats	25	75	32	68
Republicans	93	7	83	17
Independents	60	40	51	49
Catholics	50	50	55	45
Protestants	67	33	67	33
Union Members	43	57	51	49
Non-Union Members	66	34	61	39

Source: CBS News Election Day Survey[b]

[a] The tabled figures are based solely on Nixon and McGovern voters. The approximately 2 percent of voters who voted for Schmitz and other candidates are eliminated.

[b] Based on voters from a national sample of 17,405. Regions based on standard Census Bureau definitions.

the Midwest, substantial variations in electoral group behavior are apparent in 1972 despite the masking effect of a landslide election. As can be seen by inspection, Eastern labor unionists split their vote evenly between Nixon and McGovern, while Midwest rank and file labor voters heavily favored McGovern by a margin of 57 percent to 43 percent.[1] The analyses in preceding chapters indi-

1.   It should be noted that while gross regional differences were not large in regard to the Nixon vote (58% in the Midwest vs. 56% in the East), the differences between component group support were substantially greater. Variations in regional group support were even greater outside the urban belt. For example, Southern union support (66% Nixon) deviated greatly from national norms, and Southern Catholic support varied in the opposite direction (65% McGovern).

cated that liberal political values could not account for these voting patterns because Midwestern unionists were not more liberal but less so—and yet still supported the outspokenly liberal Democratic candidate George McGovern to a greater extent than their more liberal Eastern counterparts.

Close examination of Table 10 does point toward other factors, i.e., unique "party" influences, that suggest alternative explanations for such regional differences. Looking at the voter responses to the candidates, we see that Republicans in both regions were far more loyal to their party than Democrats, not an unexpected circumstance when one considers that the election was a Republican landslide. But the more illuminating aspect of the data is, rather, the regional differences found among partisan groups—both Democrats and Republicans—with regard to loyalty to their traditional party. Democrats in the East are more likely to defect from their party than Midwestern Democrats are, and the same is true of Eastern Republicans.

The greater overall looseness of party loyalty in the East, i.e., greater crossover voting among key groups, is best explained by a marked difference in the *basis of party competition* in the two regions and the "pulling power" of whatever party loyalty still exists. The party symbols appear to possess different political properties in the two regions, differences that seem to hold the voters more tightly to their avowed party in the Midwest than in the East.[2]

ELITES, NOMINATIONS, AND REGIONAL
SUB-SYSTEMS

The greater party loyalty in the Midwest cannot be attributed to wider differences in rank and file partisan opinion, for as Figures C and D have shown, the attitudinal distance between Republicans and Democrats is, if anything, greater in the East, particularly on

2. Note also the wide regional differences in Independent voting, keeping in mind that those Independents who do not vote are already excluded.

racial issues. What can account for substantial regional differences within key groups are the dynamic relationships between party rank and file and party elites in those regions, i.e., between mass groups of voters and the leadership stratum of the political parties. The specific activities of regional party elites,[3] it will be seen, can induce substantial variations both in the statewide power of party loyalty and change group voting patterns even at the presidential level.

This alternative thesis, one that focuses on elite influence in establishing candidate differences between the parties, rather than on those differences existing between rank and file partisans, offers much additional explanatory power. The important variable for our purposes, then, is not the attitudinal distance between partisans but rather the political distance between the candidates of each party and the key groups in the electorate—i.e., the *candidate distance*. Above and beyond any platform or stated party principles, then, the "meaning" of the party to the electorate is largely derived from successful candidates who articulate and dramatize political priorities and develop, in consequence, a cluster of values that comes to form the *perceived* meaning of the symbol "Republican" and "Democrat" to the population at large. Therefore, the "pull" of party affiliation, whatever its independent power, is generally weaker in a region where the two parties' candidates (and therefore the parties) are *perceived* to be closer together in political meaning—regardless of the cleavage between the political values of the mass of Republican and Democratic voters themselves.[4]

3. The term "party elites" will be used interchangeably with "activists" and denotes those political influentials who express themselves in or through party politics. Quite obviously there are many gradations of influence even within this stratum. In addition, the terms "attentive public," or "special public," are used to define that part of the general public that is particularly alert and responsive to communications from elites that involve certain specific interests and issues. See V. O. Key, Jr., *Public Opinion and American Democracy* (New York: Knopf, 1967), p. 536.
4. Of course, this concept is of more limited application in the South where the discontinuity between national and state voting patterns is

Specifically, the intra-party dynamics of the Republican Party in the East enable party elites (activists) to nominate successful candidates who are far more liberal in political values than the center of Republican mass opinion and thus narrow the perceived party differences. As a result, the decreased distance between alternative candidates in *statewide* politics consistently weakens the strength of party loyalty *in general* by minimizing symbolic party differences, and this weakness is then carried over to a certain extent to presidential elections.

Applying this thesis, for example, to working-class voters (labor unionists), the liberal personal positions of Eastern Republican candidates are perceived by union voters as not much different from those of the Democratic candidates, and, as a result, they learn to associate the term "Republican" with the social welfare position of the Republican candidates rather than the more conservative values held by rank and file Republicans. Consequently, the narrowing of perceived party differences on social welfare issues reduces the Democratic candidate's normal advantage on these traditional cleavages important to most organized workers. As a result, working-class interests are not perceived to be as firmly anchored to one party (the Democratic) in the states of the East as they are in the Midwest.

A full test of the theory of *candidate distance* requires some measurement of the values and attitudes of state-wide Democratic and Republican candidates in the East and Midwest. We need to ask whether Democratic and Republican candidates in the East are more alike on objectively defined criteria than Democratic and Republican candidates in the Midwest. Ideally, to test the candidate distance theory, we should have available candidate scores on the operational liberalism spectrum as we have for rank and file partisans of the two major parties.

Although not identical to the operational liberalism spectrum, the COPE rating developed by the political arm of the AFL-CIO

---

much greater and a fully developed two-party system is not yet operative on state-wide bases.

reflects attitudes toward a similar core of domestic programs and issues and is, for present purposes, a good measure of candidate distance. Not only is the core of issues involved in the COPE ratings comparable to the operational liberalism scale, but the COPE

TABLE 11. Labor Welfare Liberalism[a] of U. S. Senators from 1964 to 1972 by Key Geographic Regions[b] and Political Party

	Republicans[c]		*Democrats*	
		%		%
East	Brooke	94	Dodd	90
	Weicker	57	Ribicoff	94
	Saltonstall	40	Kennedy	100
	Case	96	Williams	97
	Javits	90	Clark	90
	Keating	80	Pastore	70
	Scott	77	Pell	97
	Schweiker	100		
	Goodell	91		
	Average Score	81	Average Score	91
		%		%
Midwest	Percy	93	Stevenson	89
	Dirksen	39	Douglas	90
	Griffin	50	Bayh	92
	Saxbe	35	Hartke	95
	Taft	25	Hart	97
			McNamara	90
			Lausche	60
			Young	82
			Nelson	100
			Proxmire	78
	Average Score	48	Average Score	87

a As measured by average COPE scores during 1964–72.

b Senators are those representing the same urbanized states of the regions noted in Harris Urban-Suburban Survey.

c James Buckley is omitted since he was not nominated, appointed, or elected as a Republican.

rating is itself an evaluation of voting positions by an organization representing the very group whose defections we seek to understand.[5]

Table 11 presents a comparison of U.S. Senators—Democratic and Republican, in the East and Midwest—with respect to their COPE ratings during the period 1964–1972. What we find is that the voting records of Republican Senators in the East clearly reflect a much greater orientation toward more liberal socio-economic labor concerns than is the case among Midwestern Republican Senators.

Midwestern Republicans have a mean COPE score of only 48 percent—voting "right" by labor standards less than half the time—compared to a mean score of 81 percent for their fellow Republicans in the East, a difference of over 30 percent. On the other hand, Democratic Senators in the two regions are almost fully in line with labor preferences on domestic programs (87% in the Midwest and 91% in the East).

In addition to the COPE comparison of Republican Senators from the two regions, another comparison of senatorial voting behavior was developed on key votes on racial issues (racial liberalism), since it is conceivable that greater conservatism on racial issues by Republican candidates rather than liberalism on nonracial social welfare issues could directly account for defections from the Democrats among labor unionists. However, as Table 12 demonstrates, Eastern Republican Senators have not been more conservative on race than Midwestern Republican Senators, but rather have been considerably more liberal (92% to 54%), and as liberal as the Democrats in either region.

5. Whereas other rating systems of the parties in Congress include votes on foreign policy, defense spending, and other non-social welfare issues, the COPE rating system largely avoids these issues. Rather, the COPE ratings primarily emphasize issues in the areas of programmatic welfare funding—such as education, health, housing and the economy—as well as matters of direct importance to union concerns such as minimum wage and unemployment insurance.

TABLE 12.   Racial Liberalism[a] of U. S. Senators from 1964 to 1972 by Key Geographic Regions[b] and Political Party

	Republicans[c]		Democrats	
		%		%
East	Brooke	100	Dodd	100
	Weicker	75	Ribicoff	93
	Saltonstall	100	Kennedy	100
	Case	100	Williams	86
	Javits	100	Clark	83
	Keating	100	Pastore	78
	Scott	80	Pell	86
	Schweiker	77		
	Goodell	100		
	Average Score	92	Average Score	89
		%		%
Midwest	Percy	90	Stevenson	75
	Dirksen	66	Douglas	100
	Griffin	45	Bayh	92
	Saxbe	37	Hartke	100
	Taft	33	Hart	100
			McNamara	100
			Lausche	50
			Young	100
			Nelson	71
			Proxmire	80
	Average Score	54	Average Score	87

[a] As measured by percent roll-call votes on pro-Black issues. See Appendix B, Note 8, for specific roll-call votes included.

[b] Senators are those representing the same urbanized states of the regions noted in Harris Urban-Suburban Survey.

[c] James Buckley is omitted since he was not nominated, appointed, or elected as a Republican.

The data show that during a period of intense racial conflict (1964–72), one that encompassed critical votes on civil rights, housing discrimination, Black economic opportunity, and school busing, Republican Senators in the East did not reflect the conservative views of their Republican rank and file in that region but continued their consistently liberal racial record.[6] Overall, these findings support the thesis that political partisans, especially rank and file Eastern Republicans, do not directly or proportionately translate their political preferences into statewide candidates with like attitudes. Rather, it seems that dynamic intra-party activities of the various activists and their special publics manage to produce candidates other than what we might expect in a theoretically pure process, where the candidate choice reflects the partisans' views. The choices of relatively liberal candidates by Republicans with presumably more conservative political values suggest that Republican Party elites have been able effectively to manage intra-party competition to their own philosophical and political advantage.[7]

The political effect of these relatively liberal Republican state candidates in the East is to diminish the inter-party differences between candidates and, over a period of time, change the cluster or constellation of meaning that the voter attaches to the very political symbol "Republican" itself. Thus, what is strongly suggested by the evidence is that the relative lack of voting division on a *class basis* in the East is, to a certain extent, the result of working-class people not perceiving Republican candidates as their political opposition, even though Republican rank and file partisans themselves are opposed to many union-cherished political values.[8]

6. This does not mean that individual Republican Senators could not benefit from the racial backlash following Democratically sponsored "Great Society" programs that were *perceived* by Whites to favor Blacks. It does mean, however, that Eastern Republicans did not overtly align themselves (and consequently the party) with anti-Black policies.

7. The development of the Conservative Party in New York indicates an effort by the under-represented conservatives to gain greater leverage in the selection of the Republican Party candidate—either by their co-endorsement of the Republican candidates or by running a Conservative candidate of their own in the general election.

8. This statement is not meant to underestimate the importance of contextual factors, i.e., the socio-economic setting, that may heighten or diminish working-class sensibilities. My proposition, rather, is that political elites within the parties can do much to reduce, and conversely exacerbate, the different types of cleavages that exist.

In the Midwest, on the other hand, intra-party forces have brought state-wide nominations to candidates who are very conservative Republicans, and they are perceived by the union electorate at large, as well as the labor leadership, as more clearly against working-class political interests. From the COPE ratings in Table 11 it can be seen that the political distance between Democratic and Republican Senators in the Midwest is very wide on COPE issues of domestic welfare, and this factor accentuates, rather than attenuates, the political differences between the symbols "Republican" and "Democrat" in the eyes of the union rank and file. The wide differences in COPE scores also affords Midwestern union leadership with clearer evidence than that available to Eastern union leadership with which to politicize the membership at large. Voting Republican is a small, almost negligible step for a labor unionist in the East, but a major decision in the Midwest where the label "Republican" has serious anti-working-class overtones.

Other important data help support the conclusion that relates candidate distance to potential defection among operationally liberal union voters and labor elites in the East. In New Jersey, for example, the nomination of generally liberal Republicans has helped to fragment the already divided leadership of the major unions still further. Prior to the merger of the AFL and CIO in 1955, the gubernatorial elections found CIO unions bolting to endorse the Republican candidate, Alfred Driscoll, in 1949—only to be followed in 1953 by the AFL unions jumping from the Democratic candidate to Republican Paul Trost.

Even after the merger, solid endorsements of the state Democratic candidates have been the exception rather than the rule, as the industrial unions continue to maintain a separate political council, one that endorses candidates independent of COPE activities.[9] Democratic Governor Richard Hughes and Senator Harrison

---

9. Data on the political divisions within New Jersey union leadership were made available by Joel R. Jacobson, former Director of Community

Williams of New Jersey received almost unanimous support in their individual election campaigns, while Republican Senator Clifford Case has frequently received labor endorsements by a number of important unions. In fact, he received the official endorsement of the AFL-CIO in the 1972 campaign (no doubt connected with his very high COPE rating established during his Senate career), in spite of the fact that his opponent was a former union official.

The undercutting of labor leadership support for state Democrats has been an effective strategy by some Republican candidates in Pennsylvania (Senator Richard Schweiker received the state AFL-CIO endorsement in 1974) and especially in New York, where Senator Jacob Javits has made his voting record on concerns of organized labor all but indistinguishable from Democrats.[10] Nelson Rockefeller, at the gubernatorial level, had strong union support in all of his election campaigns, and his career offers in retrospect an almost larger-than-life example of how a candidate may personally alter the meaning of the political term "Republican" from the perspective of labor unionists.

Rockefeller's massive building and road projects provided him with a "New Deal spender" image among the building trades and other related unions, and his constant wooing of labor frequently induced other unions to come to his support in one campaign after another throughout his career. Although Rockefeller in his last years as governor moved away from some of his earlier liberal positions, his strength with the labor movement, both organizationally and within the rank and file, was demonstrated repeatedly in his unprecedented four elections to the governorship of New York.

Governor Rockefeller's personal efforts in attracting labor support were well known among union leaders, and one especially observant unionist described the personal element in this way:

Relations, United Automobile Workers, Region 9, Cranford, New Jersey.
10. Senator Javits's COPE score was 90 percent in 1972; Schweiker's, 100 percent.

One part is straight ego massage—invitations to intimate din-
ners at the Executive Mansion and at least one big bash a year
where the Governor gets his picture taken with his arm around
you—but that wouldn't do it alone even with a plutocrat like
Rockefeller putting on the buddy act.[11]

This same observer, pointed to the two important elements
that have made Rockefeller's wooing of labor so successful—his
consistent support for large-scale public works programs that has
been less typical of Republicans than Democrats, and, significantly,
his clear support for liberalization in the fields of state minimum
wage, workmen's compensation and unemployment insurance—
areas which have been the traditional concerns of unionists and
Democrats alike. In this respect, former Governor Rockefeller remains a clear example of a Republican candidate personally alter-
ing the basis of labor's perception of the meaning of the symbol
"Republican," and, as a result, weakening the relative pulling
power of the symbol "Democrat" to members of organized labor.

PARTY SYMBOLS AND ELECTORAL DECISIONS

The evolution, or mutation, of the meaning of the Republican
party symbol through the nomination of liberal candidates is a
process of state politics that requires more than just one or two
elections to effect. Even though individual Republican candidates
may appeal to typically Democratic voters in specific state elections, change of *party preference* is, as we have seen, a slow and
long-term process that may lag substantially behind actual voting
choices.

In order to investigate further the important linkage between
labor, state party symbols, and presidential coalitions, a look
should be taken at regional state-wide voting patterns of union
members. Our earlier findings (Table 9) had indicated a modest

11. Quoted in A. H. Raskin, "Friend in the White House?" *New York Times,* December 4, 1972, p. 39.

TABLE 13. Statewide Party Vote of Union Members and Non-members in Eastern and Midwestern Suburbs

	Midwest		*East*	
	Union Members	*Non-Union Members*	*Union Members*	*Non-Union Members*
(Sample Sizes)	(117)	(179)	(84)	(200)
Usual Vote In State-Wide Elections				
Democratic	56%	34%	31%	29%
Republican	17%	37%	30%	37%

Source: Harris Suburban Survey

Democratic registration advantage (49% to 36%) among union members in the Eastern suburbs, a Democratic advantage that melted away at the level of presidential voting. Table 13, which presents statewide voting behavior, suggests that suburban union support at the state level in the East is significantly diminished as well, offering additional evidence of the interaction between state party politics and the eventual defections among certain key groups in the presidential coalition.

We have seen earlier that suburban union members in the East tend to lean more to Republican presidential candidates, and here we see that they also vote for Republican *statewide* candidates as often as they do for Democratic candidates.[12] These data, encompassing the suburbanized East, demonstrate the weakness of state Democratic support among labor (31% Democratic, 30% Republican) and is in sharp contrast to Midwestern statewide vot-

12. While suburban unionists are only part of the total union membership, they now represent approximately 55 percent of the unionists in Eastern metropolitan areas and about 50% in the Midwest (Harris Urban-Suburban Survey).

ing patterns where Midwestern unionists (registering with a substantial three to one Democratic preference) tend to vote just as strongly Democratic in statewide elections (56% Democratic, 17% Republican), offering evidence that the statewide conflict between Republican and Democratic candidates has a role in weakening the close association between labor and the Democratic Party at the presidential level. As statewide candidates personally help to bend party symbols into new meanings, new relationships develop between elements of the former coalition, both in the mass coalition and among political elites. A liberal Republican candidate in the East tends, for example, to weaken both mass and elite support among organized labor for the Democratic Party, blurring normally favorable linkages with the Democrats and bringing about a looser relationship between labor and Democrats even at the presidential level.

THE FEDERAL NATURE OF ELECTORAL CHANGE

There is no doubt that there are aspects of state politics, certain issues, and personalities, that may have little to do with presidential politics—certainly there are elements of independent influence at both levels in the federal system. But as we have seen, national coalitions are nevertheless intimately linked to state and local politics, particularly where a fully developed two-party system exists at all levels, and conflict can move up and down the different levels at which the party functions in the federal system.[13]

The party affiliation of key groups in the electorate is itself an allegiance determined in part by identification with local as well as national party symbols. At one extreme, of course, is the South where one's party affiliation possesses much more "local" than national political content, particularly with regard to the Democratic

13. See Duane Lockard, *New England State Politics* (Chicago: Regnery, 1959); John H. Fenton, *Midwest Politics* (New York: Holt, Rinehart and Winston, 1966).

Party. The strength of Democratic Party affiliation and voting in the local and state coalitions in the South is in marked contrast to the strong presidential support given by these same Southern voters to Republican presidential candidates over the last two decades—with Democratic presidential candidates failing to win a popular presidential majority in any Southern state after 1964. As a result, a major region exists where local-state party coalitions are largely unlike the coalitions at the presidential level, possessing little federal party interaction within each party.[14]

The other regions of the country, however, possess party systems which, while still possessing independent features, provide many more linkages between national/state/local party coalitions, and, consequently, there is greater consonance between national and local party affiliation. In the East, as we have seen, a decline in mass class cleavages, probably related in part to the political economy of the region, has been greatly exaggerated by the activities of Republican state party candidates, whose personal positions have dulled traditional Democratic advantages in class involved issues, and modified the affiliation and voting behavior of key groups both at the state and at the presidential level.

In the Midwest, on the other hand, the *distance* between state-wide party candidates has sustained class-oriented party politics and, as a result, New Deal class cleavages have tended to remain more powerful in party politics, permeating presidential as well as state coalitions. Republican candidates, the visible representations of the party, still pose strong opposition on the classic lines of social welfare activism vs. individualism, and this tends to suppress to some extent the shift to Republicanism by traditional labor Democrats along new lines of conflict such as race and foreign policy. Therefore, even though the Democratic Party has been perceived as more likely to speed racial integration, and in spite of the fact that labor unionists in the Midwest have more anti-Black attitudes,

14. Even this may be changing as two-party conflict increases, although the interaction of parties at the different levels is far below that of the regions with long established two-party systems.

labor has nevertheless tended to remain relatively more loyal to the Democratic Party in the Midwest at the state level *and* at the presidential level in both the 1968 and 1972 elections. The class basis of politics has remained stronger in that region, and appears to have moderately suppressed the rising racial backlash—at least to some extent.[15]

The basis of political conflict, aided and encouraged by the choices of Republican Party elites and candidates, has thus been maintained along more traditional class lines of party politics in the Midwest, whereas in the East class-oriented issues no longer clearly divide the candidates of one party from the other (although they still split rank and file partisans) and consequently leave the basis of specific electoral cleavages and party defections to other important but less traditional issues, e.g., character, efficacy, corruption, or race. As a result, while Republican candidates may not overtly capitalize on intense racial conflict, the absence of positive Democratic advantages along traditional cleavage lines can still stimulate defections without much visible Republican effort.

While the following chapters will show that race has probably become the single most threatening cross-cutting issue for the Democrats, for the present it suffices to note that even "race" is in reality a series of issues that is filtered in the different regions of the country through other political cleavages of varying strengths. The relatively greater "class" meaning possessed by the symbol Democrat in the Midwest, for example, tends to strengthen party loyalty and acts as a suppressant for labor defections there, despite greater conservatism in political values—indicating that it is not conflict alone but the perceived priority and relative intensity of conflict that critically determines key voting defections in a federal party system.[16]

15. The anti-working-class image of Republicans is probably responsible for labor unionists defecting to Wallace over racial issues in the Midwest and to the Republican candidate in the East over similar issues. These varying responses over racial issues will be taken up in greater detail in Chapter 6.

16. See E. E. Schattschneider, *The Semi-Sovereign People,* pp. 62–77.

PARTY LINKAGES

In the preceding chapters the nature and variability of change among key Democratic support groups have been examined in a variety of contexts—most notably along community lines, i.e., urban/suburban, and by region. While socio-economic, religious, and other regional variables are indeed broad shapers of political conflict, the evidence points to the fact that the parties themselves play a vital—though still obscure—part in the political process, one that is in certain ways independent of these sociological variables. Although reflecting the workings of socio-economic and political change, the parties nevertheless remain a vital, dynamic, and independent force in the process of change.

This "party effect" is most closely linked to *nomination politics* within each party, a process which filters, shapes, and even distorts internal political conflict inside the parties, and consequently affects the subsequent shape and range of choice for the electorate as a whole. In this process the internal dynamics of each party, particularly the role of statewide elites and their special publics, is of critical importance in forming the dimensions and intensity of party conflict and hence the loyalty among key groups even at the national level.

In the 1950s V. O. Key's examination of American state politics stressed the growing impact of national politics on state politics, pointing to increasing national influences on state political coalitions.[17] In recent years, however, his findings have sometimes been employed by scholars whose national and international interests have led them seriously to underestimate the critical feedback of state and local conflicts into the national party system. The importance of the *export* of state and local perceptions of conflict to the national arena of presidential politics and its importance in en-

17. V. O. Key, Jr., *American State Politics: An Introduction* (New York: Knopf, 1955), pp. 246–54.

couraging or discouraging defections from the national coalition make Key's own warning worth repeating:

> This discussion of the impact of the position of the state vis-a-vis the nation upon the internal structure of state politics should not obscure the fact that in various ways the form and pattern of state politics have their national effects. . . . The states as substantial political entities in the federal system, develop party structure which must be founded on the cleavages peculiar to each state. Within the national party system these peculiarities may project themselves upon the national leadership of the party.[18]

In line with Key's suggestion that national and state politics are not separable, the data introduced in these first chapters indicate that state conflicts, both inter-party and intra-party, have important political ramifications that reach deep into the key components of eventual presidential coalitions. The analysis of the data has suggested the important influence of candidate distance in reducing the general pull of party loyalty by weakening traditional party distinctions. As the candidates *personalize* and *redefine* the meaning of political symbols, party identification loses consistent independent influence over the behavior of key groups in national as well as state coalitions.

The impact of state party dynamics on presidential coalitions is by no means limited to the important but indirect role of statewide candidate distance, since the power of state party elites and special publics to shape the dimensions of conflict penetrates far beyond state cleavages—directly into the national party arena itself. Besides their role in shaping state political symbols, the very intra-party dynamics that produce statewide nominations are themselves of vital importance in providing elites and publics for national intra-party competition, i.e., for delegates to a party's presidential nominating convention.

Since the wresting of the presidential nomination comes from gaining a majority of state delegate votes, the impact of successful

18. *Ibid.*, p. 51.

political activists is usually directly felt at the national conventions. As Munger and Blackhurst's analysis of voting preferences by state delegation at the national conventions has shown, state and regional party elites do indeed press their own concept of party "meaning" by voting for the presidential candidate who appeals to their definition of the party.[19] As a result state leadership elites have, with the exception of the 1972 Democratic convention, powerfully injected their politics into the formation of national party choices by shaping the nomination process.

As critical participants in the national party arena, state elites and publics make a further impact on coalitional change among national support groups. In helping to shape the alternative presidential choices available to the electorate as a whole, these and other competing elites provide new national distance between the parties' two presidential candidates, new and nationally perceived meanings of the parties' symbols, and, consequently, new political grounds for both loyalty and defection among traditional supporters.

19. Frank Munger and James Blackhurst, "Factionalism in the National Conventions, 1940–1960: An Analysis of Ideological Consistency in State Delegation Voting," *Journal of Politics,* 27 (1965), 375–94.

II

*The Dynamics of
National Intra-Party
Power*

5

The Changing Democratic
Electorate and Elite Factionalism

The development and persistence of a two-party system throughout American politics is an historical fact of great importance in
understanding the dynamics of the political parties. The causes of
this phenomenon may be partly explained by historical factors, e.g.,
the persistence of original forms resulting from the early dualistic
cleavages presented to the young nation or from the existence of a
broad consensus on fundamental beliefs. Other institutional factors are probably even more important in promoting party duality
—for instance, the Constitutional mandate of single-member districts and plurality elections, which, unlike proportional representation, offers no share of power with political defeat.[1]

At the highest level of party power, the presidency, unlike a
multi-party cabinet, cannot be parceled out among a number of
smaller parties, and consequently the election for that post is like
the winner-take-all aspect of a single member district. These factors—historical, consensual, and institutional—all help to explain

1. See V. O. Key, Jr., *Politics, Parties and Pressure Groups,* pp. 207–10,
and E. E. Schattschneider, *Party Government* (New York: Holt, Rinehart and Winston, 1942), pp. 65–98.

the persistence of the two-party system. What precise weight each factor might appropriately be assigned in its effect on channeling conflict into two major parties is not, however, the focal point of this analysis; however, the existence of a two-party system does relate to how the overall system affects the *intra-party dynamics* of both major parties as they compete for political dominance.

Having to work through the limitations of a two-party presidential structure makes unique demands upon an American party that are unlike those generated by a multi-party system with unitary executive and legislative departments. In the American system, an important component element of a national coalition, one that might become a party of its own in a multi-party system, is forced to compromise its interests with other factions *before* a candidate is selected. Thus we see that the important position granted the candidate in a presidential two-party system forces back upon the majority party the necessary requirement of *prior* internal reconciliation of important factions, a reconciliation that is otherwise accomplished externally and after candidate selection by parties in a multi-party system.

Further, the reconciliation of the different factions or interests within the American presidential system is made without a reasonably precise knowledge of the actual strength of each interest in the party's electorate at large. Although the presidential primaries do give some indication of relative factional strength in the party's mass base, the distortions made by the unique mobilizing abilities, financial strength, and personal qualities of the different candidates tend to prevent direct knowledge of specific factional power within the party as a whole. Whereas each major interest in a multi-party system can test its actual strength in the electorate, in the American two-party system this test is only a crude assessment made by party elites.

In addition, most support groups in the American electorate are neither totally cohesive nor consistent in support from one presidential election to the next, as both parties seek and gain at least some support from most large voting interests. The success of one party in the general election can thus bring important changes in the relative power position of various factions in the other party, and, particularly in times of rapidly changing electoral core groups, this makes the evaluative assessments by political elites within the party extremely difficult.

How the two major parties compete with each other at the elite and mass levels has received much attention from political analysts. What the candidate of one party does strategically vis-à-vis the other party's candidate has been the subject of much political commentary: "The Republicans have captured the ethnic vote," "President Nixon has won over the union vote," and other such views emphasize the areas of conflict *between* the two major parties. However, these analyses of inter-party competition have tended to obscure a factor of growing political importance, namely, that *intra-party* competition in the last ten to fifteen years has become, as we shall see, a more dynamic factor than inter-party competition in determining the subsequent changes in presidential coalitions among the electorate at large.

For perspective, we need only to remind ourselves that in all three of the last presidential elections—Goldwater in 1964, Humphrey in 1968, and McGovern in 1972—the very political dynamics involved in nominating the losing candidate made a presidential election victory very difficult, if not impossible. In 1964 it was the Rockefeller-Goldwater clash that produced deep internal cleavages that were manifested in the ensuing election, divisions that turned many lesser Republican candidates, elites, as well as Independents away from the presidential candidate. Again, in the nomination campaigns of 1968 and 1972, the inability of Democratic elites and activists to reconcile themselves internally resulted in nominees whose convention victories came at a perilously high price—both of the victorious Democratic nominees started their post-convention campaigns in serious trouble with the electorate at large, including a large fraction of their own traditional followings.[2]

2. It is noteworthy that only after these three conventions did the newly nominated losing candidate drop in his popularity ratings with the

As we shall shortly discover, however, the intensity and divisiveness of intra-party competition has not struck both parties with the same impact. For, while there are internal developments that are shared by both parties, it is within the Democratic "Sun" party that the changing nature of intra-party competition has had the more dramatic and significant effects. The individual party universes of each of the two major parties contain different sets of elites, different clusters of supporters in their partisan electorate, and unique interactions between these elements—and, importantly, different "rules of the game" for the presidential nomination. Although broadly constrained by inter-party relationships, the internal dynamics of each party differ sharply and have a life very much their own.

CHANGING ELECTORAL CORES AND
PARTY ELITE INTERACTION

The outcome of intra-party competition to select the presidential candidate has become, to an increasing extent, dependent on the ability of competing elites to mobilize their publics in intra-party contests. In intra-party contests, particularly primaries, low voter interest and the absence of voting "cues" (such as a party symbol offers in a general election) give even greater power to elites who can move their followers to the polls.[3] Particularly for the Democratic Party, new elites and their attentive publics have moved forcefully into popular intra-party conflict and have pressed upon the leadership the necessity of reconciling a great number of new conflicting demands in large-scale public competition. For example, in the 1972 Democratic convention, 66 percent of all delegates were chosen in presidential primaries compared to only 41

---

electorate at large. Normally, after nomination exposure, a significant gain occurs.
3. In 1968, only fifteen states had primary elections for convention delegates; in 1972, twenty-two states held primary elections.

percent in 1968, and certain scholars have suggested that in the future it is unlikely that candidates who enter no primaries can ever be nominated.[4]

The rise in the intensity and fierceness of party factionalism was clearly manifested in the pre-convention primaries and in the conventions themselves in both the 1968 and 1972 Democratic campaigns. To a great extent the sources of divisiveness were due to problems—specifically the Vietnam War and urban-racial conflict—that were not easily resolvable, but in part they were also the result of a growing belief among insurgent Democratic forces that a new winning coalition of Independents, sympathetic Republicans, and "New Politics" Democrats[5] would be available to an insurgent candidate after the nomination. For insurgent Democratic elites in particular, looseness across party lines and the presence of large numbers of Independents only discouraged efforts to make an internal reconciliation, the assumption being that either newly enfranchised voters, Independents, or defectors from the Republican coalition would more than make up for internal losses and subsequently form the nucleus of a new majority coalition.

In the convention of 1968, even though a grudging formal reconciliation of most factions was accomplished, the political costs of internal warfare among Democratic political elites was paid for by heavy defection among disturbed Democrats in the mass, and after the 1972 convention, even the appearance of formal elite reconciliation, particularly with large segments of organized labor, was impossible to accomplish.

4. See, for example, Austin Ranney, "Changing the Rules of the Nominating Game," in James O. Barber, ed., *Choosing the President* (New York: Columbia University Press, 1974), p. 87.
5. This term refers to the insurgent Democratic elites and their attentive publics that challenged the control of the convention by regular Democratic organizations in 1968, and won the nomination in 1972. More ideologically oriented, this broadly defined group of the young, affluent "liberals" (many from the suburbs) and other party reformers have much in common with the "amateur Democrats" described by James Q. Wilson, *The Amateur Democrat: Club Politics in Three Cities* (Chicago: University of Chicago Press, 1966), pp. 2–16 and 126–63.

To a significant extent, the growing instability among different elites and their publics within the Democratic coalition has had its roots in the rapidly changing contributions made by different key support groups in the electorate at large. As certain traditional Democratic groups of the past, such as Southerners, have contributed less and less to the presidential coalition, the elites of other contributing groups (e.g., labor) have responded by seeking to expand their role in determining the presidential candidate, because their supporters "delivered the goods." And while knowledge of which groups of voters make the more important electoral contribution to a coalition does not in itself stir activity among the rank and file group members, it does stimulate knowledgeable elites to seek greater power in subsequent intra-party competition.[6]

As a group's contribution to a coalition drops significantly, rival elites sense this inability to "deliver" and make claims for a more important role in the determination of the presidential candidate in subsequent nominations. Further, the weakening enthusiasm for the Democratic Party by any electoral core (e.g., among labor rank and file) not only activates opposing non-union elite claims, but the relative indifference among rank and file unionists for the party tends to weaken any counter-efforts by labor elites to stimulate their members in contested primaries, where the more intensely interested are more likely to participate.

Robert Axelrod has clearly identified the scope of significant changes in various key group contributions to the Democratic presidential coalition from 1952 to 1972.[7] His findings show the significant and rapid changes that have occurred within the Democratic vote among important voter cores, and help explain why Democratic elite relationships have become so unstable.

The data indicate that 19 percent of the Humphrey vote and

6. For an excellent analysis of political information and the relative responses of elites and mass publics, see V. O. Key, Jr., *Public Opinion and American Democracy,* pp. 536–48.
7. Axelrod, "Where the Vote Comes From," *American Political Science Review,* p. 14. 1972 results are from Axelrod's updating, "Communications," *APSR* (June 1974), p. 718.

22 percent of the McGovern vote were contributed by Blacks in the 1968 and 1972 elections compared with only 7 percent contributed to the Kennedy coalition in 1960—an increase that is significant not only in relative size but in the short period over which it developed. The union contribution to the coalition, on the other hand, has significantly declined from a high of 38 percent in 1952 to a low of 28 percent in 1968—with a slight increase in 1972 due to the shrunken overall vote for the Democratic candidate by other voters and not to increases in union/Democratic loyalty.

When 38 percent of the Democratic vote is contributed by members of organized labor as it was in 1952, the power of labor elites in determining the presidential candidate seems difficult to challenge by less important elites, and they must reconcile their preferences with those labor elites representing (at least formally) the largest single body of Democratic voters. In the period of 1940s and 1950s and early 1960s, this labor elite group shared its power, most frequently exercised as a veto power, with big city party leaders whose "machine" organizations had historically given them significant influence in the selection of a presidential candidate. To-

TABLE 14.   Contribution to the Democratic Coalition by Various Population Groups:[a] 1952–1972

| Year | % of Democratic Candidates' Total Vote Contributed by: | | |
	Blacks	Union Members	Central Cities
1952	7	38	21
1956	5	36	19
1960	7	31	19
1964	12	32	15
1968	19	28	14
1972	22	32	14

Source: Abstract from Axelrod data

    [a] The percentage of Blacks includes other non-Whites; union members are households of union members; and central cities include only the twelve largest metropolitan areas.

gether, labor/organization dominance was a strong force for internal stability.

In a certain sense, the way by which an incumbent president, Lyndon Johnson, was denied united backing by his party, against the wishes of labor and big city party leaders, adumbrated the future challenges to "regular" political dominance within the Democratic Party. In a curious way the selection of Hubert Humphrey in 1968, without running in a single primary, was perhaps both the high point and the end of clear labor/organization dominance within the Democratic Party, since partly in reaction to the closely controlled methods of nominating Humphrey, great pressures for major changes in the "rules of the game" at future conventions were generated and ultimately accepted.

The power of the big city boss was, of course, enhanced in many cases by the various "closed" methods of selecting delegates to the Democratic national convention, but his power was nevertheless anchored politically in the important large Democratic majorities gained in the big cities. As Table 14 shows, however, the big city contribution to the Democratic coalition has also declined significantly in importance over the preceding twenty years; and as the contribution of major cities dropped to only 14 percent by 1972, so did the political validity of claims by urban bosses for power in determining the presidential nominee.[8] As the Democratic Party successfully became a middle-class party and the suburbs became a firm base of Democratic Party activity, increasing challenges were made against urban machine hegemony at the national party conventions. Without the troops and active workers, the urban machines' failure to deliver in presidential elections had stimulated powerful responses from other interests who sensed this declining power at the polls.

8. Mayor Richard Daley was the only major urban boss not challenged directly in a primary by 1972 Democratic candidates. His unseating came at the hands of a convention ruling that the slate-making procedures had not been properly followed.

The counter-response of internal elites to major coalitional changes in the Democratic electorate has not been the only cause of intra-party instability. Many new elites have also begun to seek expression within the Democratic Party, the intended and unintended results of the political strategies of the Kennedy and Johnson administrations. Since the visibility of demands is often a necessary prerequisite to building public support for new policies (as in Martin Luther King's civil rights demonstrations), visible new claimants can often enable the political leadership to move more quickly, supplying the need to act.[9] Certainly the spectacle of Bull Connor using dogs and fire hoses on Black children helped build necessary political support which gave greater impetus to the passage of civil rights legislation. And whether the issue was Indian rights or welfare rights, the organization of discontent was to some degree encouraged by Democratic administrations as a prerequisite to some kind of political solution.

Particularly in the Johnson administration, some of the new programs administered by the Office of Economic Opportunity were designed to awaken activity in the slums and activate new political groups. To qualify for some OEO grants, certain minorities were advised that a "consciousness" of their minority status as well as statistical claims of poverty were necessary, and the militancy and statistics were quickly supplied. While there is no doubt that much of the discontent was only waiting for an opportune moment of expression, many of the programs stimulated a degree of elite anticipation that the modest programs themselves could not hope to fulfill.

The stimuli provided by these programs further encouraged the rapidly growing militancy among Blacks, particularly the heretofore "invisible" Blacks in the urban ghettoes. Pressures from these newly aroused claimants were added to the already insistent voices of other Black activists, and together they pressed for Black

9. See Martin Luther King, Jr., *Why We Can't Wait* (New York: New American Library, 1964), pp. 46–75.

interests that ranged from larger welfare allotments to increased busing for school integration and community control of local administration. But while increased pressures from these various Black constituencies did bring some gains politically and, to a lesser extent, economically and educationally, they also aroused a fierce counter-mobilization among those working-class Whites whose relative immobility brought them into greater conflict with urban Blacks.[10]

During the period of the 1960s, another major elite force coalesced and joined the growing intra-party competition, bringing not only great intensity but superior financial resources and organizational skills. Largely focused on opposition to the Vietnam War, this new force made its challenge to the regular party elites by mobilizing behind Senator Eugene McCarthy, who became the focal point of the anti-war, anti-regular insurgency of the New Politics.

While some of the elements that were to join in the insurgency had long been involved in party politics, it seems clear that the anti-war position of the McCarthy campaign in 1968 served as the catalytic force that propelled the New Politics movement into a major position in Democratic Party politics. Since the "old politics" was identified with America's failing position in Vietnam, the old ways of party politics, domestic as well as foreign, had to give way, it was argued, to a new type of politics.

Along with his accurate assessment of the bankruptcy of American Vietnam policy, McCarthy brought to the Democrats a fresh challenge to the conduct of politics in general, perceiving a mandate that went far beyond Vietnam alone. The theme is well expressed in McCarthy's own words:

> Having judged the war in Vietnam was a mistake without precedent in our history, we were called upon not only to correct our mistake but to search out the causes and conditions

10. See, for example, George R. La Noue and Bruce L. R. Smith, *The Politics of School Decentralization* (Lexington, Mass.: D. C. Heath, 1973), pp. 225–39.

that led us into it. The time required us to make the hardest and harshest judgements about our national assumptions.[11]

Proponents of the New Politics argued, further, that pluralist notions of building a party coalition on the basis of different political interests bargaining for shares of power were to be abandoned because this method of organizing was against the common interest of all Americans—against a clear "public interest" that could not only be grasped in the ideal but could also replace the old fragmented coalitional politics at the operational level as well. Consequently, McCarthy rejected attempts to organize his own campaign around various interests and ethnic groups and met opponents' efforts to do so with disdain—the public interest was indivisible.

> I have not really become a candidate because a combination was put together in support of me. I saw a story today where one potential candidate has 26 separate committees of various kinds of Americans. I knew that Howard Johnson had 28 varieties of ice cream, but did not know that there were 26 varieties of Americans who could be combined for political purposes. I do not really have but one variety: a constituency that is a constituency of conscience.[12]

McCarthy's unwillingness to accept the competition of different groups and "types" of Americans even extended to his refusal to acknowledge the unique position of Blacks in America:

> We had to deal with straight problems which are the concern of *every* citizen in this country—simply because he is a citizen and not because he is a member of any organization or group or minority. In this speech I emphasized that I was quite prepared to speak about the injustices in our country—against Negroes and against others—and was doing so, but only in order to get all the people to accept their responsibility and not to distract people from the *common* problems which faced us.[13]

11. Eugene J. McCarthy, *The Year of the People* (New York: Doubleday, 1969), p. 162.
12. *Ibid.,* p. 318.
13. *Ibid.,* p. 162.

McCarthy's important role in shaping and propelling the New Politics faction into a major position within the Democratic Party was not limited to the 1968 intra-party struggle, for besides young protesters his campaign stimulated and mobilized vast numbers of new activists and attentive publics—many from the normally inactive suburbs—to take part in party politics for the first time. These activists, drawn heavily from the less active, non-political middle class, involved themselves in nomination politics (along with their college offspring) to an extent never approached before in past party politics. Despite failure in their immediate efforts to nominate Eugene McCarthy in 1968, their impact was to be subsequently and dramatically felt in the McGovern nomination in 1972 and, perhaps more importantly, in their role in restructuring the "rules of the game" for future Democratic politics.

NEW POLITICS, NEW DEMOCRATS, AND SUBURBANIZATION

In a certain sense the suburban Democrat has characteristically represented the broadening social basis of the postwar Democratic "Sun" coalition, a mass electorate with very little middle-class support when it became the dominant party in the 1930s. The gains in the middle class by the Democrats were not made, as Everett Ladd has pointed out, because Republican middle-class voters shifted from their earlier loyalties, but stemmed rather from Democratic success in attracting a larger share of the middle class among new emerging voters.[14]

However, this very success of the Democrats in recruiting the new, largely suburban middle-class voters has brought with it certain political problems of another kind—not in terms of weak voting loyalty by these new party adherents, but, as we shall see, in the disproportionate impact of political activists from these affluent suburbs on *intra-party* conflict. For though not as substantial in

14.   Everett C. Ladd, Jr., *American Political Parties,* p. 236.

numbers as other supporters in the Democratic national electorate, such as labor unionists and Blacks, this stratum of Democrats has come to provide a substantially disproportionate share of the political activists in critical internal party battles, as well as much needed financial resources.

Several factors seem at least partially to explain the growing power of this reform-oriented, middle-class corps in internal Democratic presidential politics. First, the social characteristics of middle-class suburban Democrats provide an excellent underpinning for political mobilization, encompassing a disproportionate share of the college-educated, professionals, and the affluent. These types of individuals, as Philip Converse has demonstrated, not only respond to issues and ideological content more readily than others, but are also more willing and able to turn their political awareness into politically effective activism.[15] And not unexpectedly, they have strongly supported the more ideological New Politics faction of the party in its challenge of "regular" organizational control of the party.

Wilson's study of insurgent "amateur Democrats" and Polsby and Wildavsky's analysis of 1964 Goldwater elites both brought increased focus on the impact of the new activist stratum in American politics. Wilson's Democratic "amateur" and Polsby and Wildavsky's Republican "purist" showed many similar approaches to the practice of politics, even while holding radically different policy positions—with the "amateur Democrats" to the left of their party's center and the Republican "purists" to the right of theirs.[16] Both

15. See Philip E. Converse, "The Nature of Belief Systems in Mass Publics," in *Ideology and Discontent,* ed. David E. Apter (New York: The Free Press, 1964), pp. 206–61.
16. See James Q. Wilson, *The Amateur Democrat*; Aaron B. Wildavsky, "The Goldwater Phenomenon: Purists, Politicians and the Two-Party System," *Review of Politics,* 27 (July 1965), 386–413; Nelson W. Polsby, "Strategic Considerations," in *The National Election of 1964,* ed. Milton C. Cummings (Washington: Brookings Institution, 1966); Nelson W. Polsby and Aaron B. Wildavsky, *Presidential Elections: Strategies of American Electoral Politics* (2nd ed., New York: Scribners, 1968), pp. 173–83.

these sets of activists maintained strong ideological orientations, and though both were desirous of winning the later general election, they were even more concerned with getting a candidate who was ideologically "right." They were both, in fact, activists with concern for programs and policies that could be clearly articulated, were little concerned with maintaining party organizational stability, and were tightly bound to their candidate by the understanding that he would not compromise the positions he had taken.

The amateur-professional dichotomy still remains a useful concept of elite analysis, particularly if it is not overextended. Soule and Clarke, for example, found only a modest amount of attitudinal distance along certain lines of liberalism and conservatism between Democratic amateurs and professionals at the 1968 convention, but reaffirmed Wilson's thesis that the *way* in which amateurs and professionals held their values—their readiness to compromise their choices—markedly differed.[17] It seems likely that at least some of the features attributed to the amateur or purist are not, in fact, intrinsic but rather are strategic responses by a group to their particular organizational situation as the usual "outgroup."[18] But it is also very important to keep in mind how quickly differences in political *style* turn into differences of *policy,* for as later chapters will show, the willingness to resist or accept compromise on certain issues can significantly affect the alternative choices available to the voter and consequently shapes the very substance of politics.

Among those elements comprising the New Politics faction (i.e., anti-war elites, the young, intellectuals, and other left-liberals), the affluent suburban Democrat was a singularly important one, for he, unlike his other political partners, possessed significant resources that were in short supply—most specifically,

17. John W. Soule and James W. Clarke, "Amateurs and Professionals: A Study of Delegates to the 1968 Democratic Convention," *American Political Science Review,* LXIV (1970), 891–98.

18. See Jeffrey L. Pressman and Denis G. Sullivan, "Convention Reform and Conventional Wisdom: An Empirical Assessment of Democratic Party Reforms," *Political Science Quarterly,* 89 (Fall 1974), 345–46.

much-needed financial and organizational resources. Indeed, one of McGovern's earliest and most accomplished political organizers, Professor Richard C. Wade, started his national fund-raising effort in the crucial New York metropolitan area by organizing clusters of McGovern financial supporters in the suburbs surrounding the city.[19] As Wade stated,

> In the race for the nomination, the McGovern strategy was anti-regular, and strongly pitched to the issue-oriented, anti-war reform elements of the Party. The typical activist, ready, willing and able to support McGovern both financially and otherwise was a suburban Democrat, mid-forties in age, children of teenage or early twenties, liberal and policy-oriented, and possessing financial resources of his own or his family's— which he was willing to put to work.[20]

Building upon Eugene McCarthy's demonstrated strength in suburban areas during the 1968 pre-nomination campaign, Wade developed his campaign base first in the suburbs and then worked his way back to the inner-city, finally defeating the resistant but ineffective urban machines in the New York primary of June 1972. "The suburbs of the major cities," Wade noted, "were a great strength of our campaigns throughout, both in terms of activists and in terms of votes."[21] And the voting results in suburban counties in the primaries demonstrated the insurgent-reform strength of McGovern in these areas. Not only did McGovern sweep the suburban counties in the concluding New York and New Jersey primaries in June of 1972, but his strength in the affluent suburbs kept him viable while he was trying to establish himself as a serious candidate in other key industrial states. In the Pennsylvania primary, for example, McGovern won 26 of his 37 delegates in the suburbs and the few affluent parts of the major cities.[22] And as CBS News' primary surveys indicated, suburban rather than urban strength

19. See Theodore H. White, *The Making of the President, 1972* (New York: Bantam, 1973), p. 172.
20. Interview with Richard C. Wade, New York City, July 2, 1974.
21. *Ibid.*
22. R. W. Apple, Jr., *New York Times,* April 27, 1972, p. 42.

was a mainstay of the McGovern campaign in other states as well.[23]

The strength of the New Politics faction in the suburbs is at least partially accounted for by the social, economic, and educational position of these Democrats, but, as one should expect, these characteristics alone do not fully explain why this faction has been able to dominate other Democrats who have perhaps even more voting potential in the suburbs, i.e., politically moderate middle-class Democrats and working-class suburban Democrats. A more complete answer seems to lie in a rather complex combination of factors. First is the high level of motivation and energy of these insurgent activists (particularly when fortified by strong national issues), features common to more ideological activists in general. This intensity factor is also critically related to a second factor—the relative weakness of the regular Democratic Party organization in the affluent suburbs.

One important element that contributes to "regular" Democratic organizational weakness in the suburbs is that suburban Democrats, unlike their Republican counterparts, have not controlled the county government in middle- and upper-middle-class suburbs for any sustained period of time. In fact, only since the early 1960s have the Democrats won any substantial number of executive offices at the county level. However, even in those areas where they have won control of the county political machinery, the minority status of Democrats in middle-class suburbs has fostered a non-partisan, non-patronage, "good government" approach, which, while sound political strategy for getting elected, limits the ability of organizational elites to build a strong party. The more affluent suburban counties, unlike those with substantial working-class suburbs, have been long-time Republican strongholds, a condition that restricts a strong partisan posture in Democratic

23.   CBS News, Primary Election Surveys. It is important, however, to remember that the suburban strength for McGovern was only a feature of *nomination* voting patterns in the Democratic Party, i.e., intra-party strength. The suburbs returned large majorities for Richard Nixon in the general elections of both 1968 and 1972.

campaigns and consequently weakens the party's organizational foundation.

Long-term dominance in any important election unit seems vital to developing strong internal organizational resources, and for the Democrats in the middle-class suburbs, traditional Republican political power has helped to weaken local Democratic Party organization. In fact, these distinctions reflecting the relative power positions between Democratic and Republican organizations are sharply framed in Dennis Ippolito's study of suburban activists, which has shown that Republican Party elites demonstrate a much stronger sense of party organizational attachment than suburban Democrats; while suburban Democrats conversely show stronger ideological, philosophical, and issue motivations than Republican activists.[24]

It is likely that the long Republican control of the political machinery and resources of suburban counties has fostered the development of more solid political organizations, for it should be remembered that until the last decade or so Republican dominance in these suburbs was almost as great as Democratic dominance in the big cities. In any case, the fact remains that Democratic suburban party organizations are generally weak at the county level, and therefore as nationally oriented New Politics elites periodically galvanize themselves to action, there is little regular organizational strength to mount against them.

Not unexpectedly, the growing effectiveness of this middle-class stratum in determining the Democratic Party's candidates has been accompanied by deepening concern among leaders of the labor/organization faction of the Democratic Party. Leaders of these less affluent, largely urban Democratic interests in the party electorate resent and fear the disproportionate power of these middle-class activists, who are able to multiply the power of their smaller electoral base in the internal contests to control the party's presidential nomination. To many labor/organization activists, the

---

24. Dennis S. Ippolito, "Political Perspectives of Suburban Party Leaders," *Social Science Quarterly*, 49 (March 1969), 800–815.

New Politics faction is viewed as divisive, non-representative of the Party as a whole, and only paradoxically powerful—possessing substantial strength in intra-party fights but unable to convert it into general election voting power.

Although not as far apart on many specific economic and social issues as the intensity of conflict would indicate, elite conflict among these two broad factions centers heavily on *how* party politics should be carried on. Bargaining among party interests, not "ideological purity" and open conflict, is seen by the labor/organization faction as the most effective way for a party to operate internally, much in the traditional "brokerage" manner of past politics. On the other hand, middle-class, New Politics elites tend to view party politics in altogether different terms, demanding a more policy-consistent, internally democratic structure, rather than an oligarchic party organization—and believing that the old accommodation style of politics has been detrimental to progress. Everett Ladd, Jr., and Charles Hadley noted this conflict over appropriate party models as follows:

> What is evident is the emergence of an activist stratum, heavily college educated and middle-class, inclined to substitute a conflict for an accommodation model, and preoccupied with the politics of issues and principles. No word ranks higher in the lexicon of party directed participants than "compromise." For the issue activists, by way of contrast, the country had paid a severe price for an excessive fealty to a politics of compromise.[25]

The reform, issue-oriented activists of the new middle class have served in many ways as a catalytic force for social change and progress, pressing the center of the party further away from its stable but status quo center. However, a high level of ideological consistency seems difficult to sustain in an omnibus two-party system

25.   Everett C. Ladd, Jr., and Charles D. Hadley, "Political Parties and Political Issues: Patterns in Differentiation Since the New Deal," Sage Professional Papers, in American Politics, Vol. 1, series 04–010 1973, p. 44.

where a single party must piece together various different "issue publics" and social groups under the same party banner. The symbol of the party can hardly be tightly defined in such a heterogeneous electorate as the Democrats encompass without eventually running the risk of significant defections by elite and mass interests that do not accept "the" definition of the party symbol.

The New Politics faction has had a major impact on the Democratic nomination processes, heightening the ideological content of intra-party conflict and forcing the party to consider in its deliberations many issues that other party interests would prefer to play down for purposes of their own, or for party unity. In addition to promoting the issue content of party policy, the reform wing has also successfully pressured the party to further "democratize" its internal procedures for nominating its presidential candidate—that is, opening the selection process by increasing the scope of participation by rank and file Democrats in presidential primaries. But the new manner of delegate selection appears largely to shift the internal advantage from the labor/organization elites of the urban working-class and ethnic voters to a new set of elites more responsive to middle-class Democrats[26]—without, as we shall see in subsequent chapters, more accurately reflecting the views of the majority of rank and file Democrats.

It is important to remember that large urban party organizations, pejoratively remembered as machines, have historically represented urban ethnic and working-class groups within the Democratic Party—regardless of how morally corrupt they have seemed to successive waves of middle-class reformers. Even though sluggish in response, open to "honest graft," and overly pragmatic, the strong party organization in the major city has been the vehicle of the less aware, less educated, and less affluent masses. It has been, as Frank Sorauf noted, "the political organization of the masses who lack the cues and information—as well as the political re-

26. See John S. Saloma and Frederick H. Sontag, *Parties for Effective Citizen Politics: The Real Opportunity* (New York: Vintage Books, 1973), p. 393.

sources of status, skills and money—to make a major impact on public decisions via other means."[27] The decline of the machine and the shrinking power of its labor ally in the internal processes of presidential politics have opened the Democratic Party to new pressures for change, many of which serve the cause of political and social progress. But at the same time its decline has disproportionately favored the interests of middle-class Democrats at the expense of working-class Democrats, and has consequently intensified the internal instability of the party.

As the traditional "brokers" of power in the presidential nomination process have given way to a more fluid system of competing elites and their attentive publics (seven of every ten delegates to the 1976 Democratic convention will be elected, not selected), the degree of leeway available for bargaining and reconciling various intra-party interests has been greatly diminished. In its place has come the restless, unstable, and dynamic interaction of conflicting electoral cores and activist corps as they seek to reflect their power in the party by determining the presidential candidate. And if the divisive 1968 and 1972 Democratic conventions demonstrated nothing else, they clearly showed that such a deeply unreconciled Democratic Party would generate a candidate likely to be rejected later by the electorate at large.

27. Frank Sorauf, *Party Politics in America* (2nd ed.), Boston: Little, Brown, 1972), p. 420.

6

Race and National Democratic Politics

From the end of the Reconstruction following the Civil War to the close of World War II, the South and the Democratic Party were tied in a unique relationship, unlike any other in American history. In this period of American politics, race as a political determinant was the essential ingredient of an unquestioning attachment that lasted, almost unbroken, from 1876 to 1944, critically shaping national as well as Southern politics. In fact, nowhere can the power of the federal linkage between state political leaders and national Democratic Party choices be seen with more clarity than here. As C. Vann Woodward described this relationship of party, region and race, "The Democrats ceased to be a party *in* the South and became the party *of* the South. Politics was a continuation of Civil War history by other means."[1]

During this period the Republican Party received the electoral votes of a Southern state in only nine out of a possible 198 instances; three occurring in 1876 and five in 1928, when Al Smith, a Catholic, was the nominee. And four of the eleven states of the

---

1. C. Vann Woodward, "The Chaotic Politics of the South," *The New York Review,* December 14, 1972, 37.

Confederacy maintained an unbroken record of Democratic loyalty throughout this period of almost seven decades.

This particular phase of racial politics ended with the presidential election of 1944, which was the last "solid South" election of the post-Depression Democratic coalition. Beginning with the presidential election of 1948, a new phase emerged in the relationship between the South and the national Democratic Party—one in which the South changed within two decades from the strongest Democratic region to the weakest from the standpoint of presidential elections. The defections in the South that began with Strom Thurmond's "walk-out" from the 1948 National Democratic convention came to provide, on balance, Republican electoral advantage in four of the next six elections from 1952 to 1972, and the dimensions of this national reordering of racial politics in the South became even more apparent in light of Barry Goldwater's significant victories made in the face of a national Democratic landslide in 1964. Goldwater obtained 49 percent of the Southern vote overall, and as one moved from the states of the "outer rim" to those of the "Black belt," Goldwater actually ran up large majorities. The very same Deep South states that had voted their "Democratic racial history" as late as the two Stevenson campaigns, had by 1964 realigned themselves with the Republican national ticket as contemporary racial politics came to dominate those of Civil War history.[2]

The new patterns of political allegiance in the South have come about not as the result of any single, sudden, or clear-cut racial position taken by the Democratic Party. Rather, they have evolved over time from a series of mass-elite responses to major socio-political pressures in American political life, some forces originating within the party system and some from without. One crucial pressure, a political stimulant coming from outside the party

2. This change in Deep South voting patterns in 1964 is seen by Walter Dean Burnham as possibly the beginning of a critical realignment. See Walter Dean Burnham, "American Voting Behavior in the 1964 Election," *American Political Science Review,* 59 (1965), 1–40.

system, was judicial action—the landmark Supreme Court decision *Brown vs. The Board of Education* in 1954—reversing the legal grounds for segregation in public education established 58 years earlier in *Plessy vs. Ferguson.* By attacking the legal foundation for "separate but equal," the *Brown* decision served as a critical catalyst that legally confronted reluctant American parties with demands for political implementation, stimulating in turn varying partisan responses that were to have an explosive impact on future party alignments.

Besides the crucial *Brown* decision, another major pressure that was to eventually affect long stable coalitional alignments was the massive movement of the Black population from the agricultural communities of the South to the urban centers of the North. Massive economic disruption, the result of a technological revolution in Southern agriculture, had created millions of unemployed rural Black farmers by the end of World War I, and a substantial part of this vast pool of impoverished Blacks was to be drawn to the North in the ensuing decades.[3] Heavily stimulated by the availability of World War II production jobs, the massive movement of Black population to the North continued throughout the decades of 1950s and 1960s, long after the initial stimulus of the war was over. The great scope of this migration can be seen most clearly by the fact that in the three decades between 1940 and 1970, the percentage of the nation's total Black population living in the South had declined from 77 percent to 53 percent, the result of a migration of almost five million Negroes.[4]

This tremendous internal migration of the Black population, unparalleled in American history, has been of great significance for the Democratic Party and, of course, for American politics in general, because in a little over a quarter of a century it has national-

3. See Gilbert Osofsky, *Harlem: The Making of a Negro-Ghetto, New York, 1890–1930* (New York: Harper & Row, 1963); also Ira Katznelson, *Black Men, White Cities: Race, Politics, and Migration in the United States, 1900–30, and Britain, 1948–68* (London; Oxford University Press, 1973), pp. 45–122.
4. See 1970 Census, *Social and Economic Status of Negroes,* p. 12.

ized racial polarity and hostility. The national Democratic Party, no longer able to contain racial issues under its traditional regional umbrella, has had to absorb the impact of spreading racial con- flict. Walter Dean Burnham has described the developing national scale as follows:

> This nationalization has had several consequences: it has de- stroyed the old bases of the Democratic Party in most of the South, at least for the time being; it has helped motivate Blacks to develop a greater sense of their own political identity, as a separate quasinational group in the United States; and it has led to a furious countermobilization by those Whites of the "great middle" who are least able to escape the Black presence by flight into the suburbs or to Private schools for their children.[5]

PARTY ELITES: RACE AND THE "RULES OF THE GAME"

The *Brown* decision and the massive migration of rural Southern Blacks to the urban North were both important catalysts in bring- ing further change to the New Deal Democratic coalition of an ur- ban North and a rural South. But no matter how important these pressures were, the ability of the Democratic Party to respond to these challenges would have been limited had not a major institu- tional "lock" on racial conflict been lifted earlier by changing the party's "rules of the game." The long standing two-thirds majority rule for the nomination of a Democratic candidate for President was finally reduced to a simple majority in 1936, and this critical change in the rules subsequently contributed to the emergence of a new and dynamic era of party and race relationships for the Demo- crats. No longer could an obstinate minority faction of party elites block the nomination of a presidential candidate with only one-

5. Walter Dean Burnham, *Critical Election, and the Mainsprings of American Politics* (New York: W. W. Norton, 1970), p. 142.

third plus one of the delegates, thereby keeping a tight hold over presidential initiative in racial matters.

Perhaps reflecting the concerns of those who feared the tyranny of the majority over important minority interests, the heavily Southern based Democratic Party had established the two-thirds majority rule at its first convention in 1832, a rule that lasted amid controversy until it was abrogated more than a century later in 1936.[6] But regardless of the origins of the rule, the protection of the racial interests of the South was without doubt an essential part of the rule's durability. The rule's political objective "was to make it certain that no candidate could be nominated except with the concurrent approval—or at least the passive consent—of most major factions within the party."[7]

More than the actual use of the rule has been its impact as a latent strategic threat to any nationally ambitious Democratic politician, i.e., in preventing rather than deciding intra-party conflict of racial import. It is important to grasp fully the great strategic power of this rule that could be used against any Democratic presidential aspirant suspected of introducing new racially loaded issues into national party deliberations; for the South and potential allies from segregated border states (Maryland, West Virginia, Delaware, Kentucky, Missouri, and Oklahoma) could well have ended the presidential aspirations of any candidate posing a threat to the status quo on race. In terms of practical political strategy, a candidate who clearly violated the tradition of keeping race a regional rather than a national issue faced the necessity of winning almost all the votes of the non-segregated states, a strategy unlikely to be adopted by serious presidential candidates. And the blank pages

6. No debate is recorded on the resolution requiring the two-thirds rule at the 1832 convention. See Richard C. Bain and Judith H. Parris, *Convention Decisions and Voting Records* (2nd ed., Washington, D.C.: Brookings Institution, 1973), p. 18.

7. Paul T. David, Ralph M. Goldman, Richard C. Bain, *The Politics of National Party Conventions* (Washington, D.C.: Brookings Institution, 1960), p. 208.

of racial history at the Democratic conventions is the greatest proof of the intimidating force of the two-thirds rule.

The potential of such minority power to block the choice of the majority was clearly established in the minds of Democratic presidential hopefuls in the early decades of the twentieth century. Woodrow Wilson, the first Democratic President of the twentieth century, benefited from this power of the minority when his rival, Speaker Champ Clark, saw his tenth-ballot simple majority finally overcome by Wilson's eventual victory on the forty-sixth ballot. The importance of the South as a political base for Wilson was shown by the humiliating segregation of hitherto unsegregated Black Federal employees during his administration. In effect, presidential opportunity for a Democrat under a two-thirds rule was inversely related to any stance by a nominee that could be considered at all pro-integration.

As a political instrument the two-thirds rule was more effective in preventing conflict from entering the party arena than it was in ending it once conflict had been initiated. After intense conflict had actually begun (particularly over candidates with strong ideological backing) the two-thirds rule had the effect of only prolonging the struggle, the worst example being the Democratic convention of 1924 which became a shambles of divisiveness and futility. This Democratic Convention debacle covered sixteen days and required 103 ballots to bring forth an uninspiring compromise candidate, John W. Davis, after an unbreakable deadlock developed between the urban, anti-prohibition forces of Al Smith and the conservative, rural, and "dry" supporters of William McAdoo.

In 1924 Al Smith had stood with urban supporters, Catholics, liberals, and other "cosmopolitans" in support of a minority plank against the Ku Klux Klan or any organization that sought to limit the civil rights of any individual on the basis of religion, birthplace, or racial origin. However, even this broad, non-specific affirmation of Constitutional rights was beaten back by anti-civil rights forces by a close vote, indicating only too clearly what the cost would be to candidates who would need to reverse this defeat and then gain a two-thirds majority to win the nomination.

The very futility of the process in 1924 was an important catalyst that forced the Democratic Party seriously to confront the question of whether a simple majority rather than a two-thirds majority was to the best advantage of the Democratic presidential party in the twentieth century. The very need to win the Presidency in a century of increasing presidential power steadily pressed upon local and state party elites the need to find a more practical way to select a candidate, and especially to select a candidate in such a manner as to preserve his later chances in the general election. In order to become a genuine national party, sectional power (or any factional minority) could not be permitted to keep such a strong and disruptive grip over national candidate choices.

With the 1924 debacle behind them, much sentiment among Democratic party elites focused on abrogating the two-thirds rule in time for the next convention. Early in 1926 the editors of the *New York Times* decided to test how much support a rule change had among party elites and polled the members of the Democratic National Committee on their positions over the rule. Among those members of the DNC replying, only eight opposed removing the two-thirds rule while twenty-four favored the change and only one was uncommitted. In addition, the leading supporters of both Smith and McAdoo at the past convention voiced their support for abrogation of the rule, and other published comments from non-committee party elites also reflected the serious intentions of party activists to prevent a disaster similar to 1924 and permit the orderly nomination of a suitable candidate of the majority.[8]

Buried among these replies by Democratic National Committee members to the poll were signs of a developing reaction among party activists that were to prove of great significance. While the majority of the committeemen from the Southern states supported continuance of the two-thirds rule, four of the eleven Southern dele-

8.   *New York Times,* May 24, 1926, 1–2.

gates replying declared in favor of changing the rule, and significantly, these four locally selected Democratic organizational leaders had taken the position publicly. The position on the minority rule that had been solidly backed by Southern Democratic politicians in the twentieth century had begun to fragment.

The optimism promoted by these responses for a rather speedy abrogation of the two-thirds rule was quickly dispelled at the 1928 convention. Al Smith's tremendous lead going into the convention permitted him to be quickly and easily selected under the old two-thirds rule, and Smith, not wanting to alienate the South further, chose not to make the rule change an issue.[9] The first major convention assault on the two-thirds rule in this century came in the challenge by the Roosevelt forces at the 1932 convention. The attempt itself failed, but the deliberations of the party activists at that convention gave strong indications of the further fragmenting of the Southern bloc's position within the national party.

In 1932, faced with no apparent racial threats but fearful of economic ruin from the devastating Depression, the South sharply divided in its support of the traditional two-thirds majority position. Economically motivated Southerners, such as Representative John Rankin of Mississippi, attempted to rally state delegation forces in favor of abrogation, only to be countered by fellow Mississippian ex-Senator John Sharpe Williams, whose urgent wire to the state delegation sought to reaffirm the traditional Southern position. His message: "Two-thirds rule has been for a century the South's defense and it would be idiotic on her part to surrender it."[10] To Williams, vigilance to preserve Southern power was necessary even when facing national economic disaster.

The tension in maintaining Southern unity revealed the growing dominance of a new political cleavage over an old one, or again

---

9.   In fact, in an attempt to placate Southern opposition Smith agreed to the holding of the convention in a state of the Confederacy. See Bain and Parris, *op. cit.,* p. 232.

10.   *New York Times,* June 26, 1932, p. 1.

in E. E. Schattschneider's words, the displacement of one political conflict by another. Rankin, for example, asserted that the rule had "long outlived its usefulness" and was no longer of use to the South. The two-thirds rule, he argued further, "was a powerful weapon in the hands of the Wall Street element which was being used to dictate the nominees and control of policies of the party."[11] Rankin did not stand alone, for he was joined by other Southern convention speakers, such as the nationally ambitious Governor Huey Long of Louisiana, who bluntly charged that important financial interests were trying to block Roosevelt by the two-thirds rule when he had the nomination already won.[12]

But the moment for change had not arrived, and the call for immediate action was finally stemmed at the 1932 convention by a fierce countermobilization by Harry F. Byrd and Carter Glass of Virginia, whose efforts brought other Southerners into strong convention opposition and brought capitulation from the Roosevelt forces. With victory close at hand, the contagiousness of further conflict, particularly the defection of Roosevelt's strong Southern support, could no longer be risked on such a matter. The principal argument that seemingly had joined both Southern and Northern opposition against the rule change at the 1932 convention was that it seemed somehow unfair to change the rules once the game and the contestants were already in action. And therefore, as the 1932 convention closed, a voice vote adopted a rules committee recommendation warning future contenders that the following convention in 1936 was to make the nomination for President a matter of a simple, rather than a two-thirds, majority.

In 1936, an estimated nine hundred delegates, backed by an enormously popular President, came to the convention prepared to lay the two-thirds rule to rest.[13] The Rules Committee finally voted 36 to 13 for abrogation, although only after assurances were given that the new rules on delegate apportionment for 1940 would give

11. *Ibid.*
12. *Ibid.*
13. *New York Times,* June 26, 1936, p. 1.

greater recognition to the solidly Democratic states—a change clearly perceived as consolation for the South.[14] By this time, the new national base of support gained by F.D.R. was of sufficient strength to override any attempted Southern opposition, for as the power base of the Roosevelt administration was spreading to all parts of the country, the relative power of the South within the Democratic Party was shrinking, and this was clearly symbolized in the final floor speech after the motion was introduced.

> Mr. Chairman, there could be no sectional issues, because no section of the United States could be injured or affronted by being subjected to the will of the majority of the Democratic National Convention. And, thank God, the Democratic Party is no longer a sectional party; it has become a great national party! And tonight *there is not one state in the Union, North, South, East or West, in which it is not only possible but probable that the ticket of Roosevelt and Garner is going to carry.*[15]

Then by a voice vote, without any floor fight whatsoever, the new rule of simple majority control over the presidential nomination was passed, making a profound change in the institutional structure of the Democratic Party—with its ramifications only dimly perceived by many of those present at the convention. The destructive divisiveness of preceding conventions, the growing democratic majoritarian spirit of party elites, the subordination of racial concerns to the more urgent political needs of a Depression trauma, and perhaps Southern overconfidence in their ability to constrain the racial issue congressionally, all combined to break an institutional "lock" that had effectively denied party access to potential civil rights inputs in the formative processes of presidential leadership, and, consequently, to national racial policy.

So long as the presidential nominee needed two-thirds of the delegates to win the nomination, the convention vote of segregated states had a strategic (though not absolute) veto over a Democratic candidate—an instrument of power sufficient to foreclose leader-

14. Bain and Parris, *op. cit.,* p. 249.
15. *Democratic National Proceedings,* 1936, pp. 192–93 (italics mine).

ship advocacy of even the most modest pro-civil rights policies and suppress the development of civil rights elites in the national party. From the end of the nineteenth century until 1928 the South had provided the only solid and continuous electoral strength for Democratic presidential candidates but at a high price—on the condition that a sectional rather than national definition of racial justice would prevail.

The nomination of Al Smith in 1928 had marked the first major step in a transfer of power within the modern Democratic Party, acknowledging that electoral strength within the party had moved from the agrarian states of the South and West to the major urban states of the East and the industrialized Midwest; a critical shift in the locus of power within the party that was finally anchored securely by Roosevelt in 1936. In that landslide election victory a new political era began, one based upon a massive new electoral realignment that in effect undermined the hegemony of Southern sectionalism. The scope of the Democratic presidential and congressional victories had deepened the national basis of the party at Southern expense, for whereas the South had been a majority faction in a minority party during the 1920s, by the 1930s it had become a minority faction in a much expanded majority party. While the South still possessed great leverage points in the Congress, a powerful and popular President with a large national base sharply reduced the implicit and explicit sanctions of the South over the national party. The broadening by Roosevelt of the national party's base through new policies of social activism together with the removal of the two-thirds rule had closed an era where the South was needed as a "concurrent majority" in the choice of Democratic presidential candidates.

The nationalizing of the Democratic Party through Roosevelt's victories, and the vast increases in presidential power granted the President to combat the Great Depression both reflected and initiated dynamic forces for political change, and in the broad sweep of social and political turbulence, a critical racial monitor over presidential choices, the two-thirds rule, was finally surrendered.

While the racial impact of the new convention rule was not to be immediate, the combination of a progressive, activist national government and new internal rules had opened the party to the dynamics of race. The "democratizing" of the Democratic Party convention by the party's elites was just the beginning, and, as we shall see, by 1948 the interaction of the party activists and their various publics made race a major issue of conflict in Democratic presidential politics. Race and racial interests were getting in the presidential party game.

ELITE STRATEGY AND THE
GROWTH OF MASS CONFLICT

With his large-scale commitments to programmatic liberalism (or operational liberalism), Roosevelt had in effect chosen the urban/liberal wing of the party over the Southern conservative bloc. But while sharp divisions did develop between these factions during the middle 1930s and early 1940s over general social welfare policies, F.D.R. did not actually extend his party's public commitment to racial welfare significantly.

Roosevelt did encourage the liberal hiring of Blacks in the lower levels of a rapidly growing bureaucracy, and also brought a number of relatively young and highly educated Blacks into the middle levels of certain aggressive bureaus; but he was very reluctant to introduce change in the racial status quo as an issue for the White electorate at large. In fact, aside from the pro-integration activities of individual Democratic personalities, the Roosevelt administration itself proposed very little directed specifically toward Black interests, not even mentioning racial inequality in the party platform until the 1940 convention. For the small but growing Black electorate at large, preference for the Democratic Party was generated, rather, by Democratic policies that had steadily improved the economic well-being of both Blacks and Whites during the post-Depression recovery.

It would be fair to say that almost all the specifically racial gains made during the Roosevelt administration were accomplished by elite pressure, Black and White, rather than by any party appeal to the White or Black electorate at large; and specific gains, such as Executive Order 8802 in June 1941 banning discrimination in defense industries, were the result of Black activist pressure on the administration—notably, A. Philip Randolph's threat to lead a massive Black march on Washington if the Order was not issued.[16]

Taken as a whole, specific Black gains during the Roosevelt years were very small, for the Southern wing not only had important institutional power in Congress, but was still a large block in the Electoral College, and fears of close elections in 1940 and 1944 effectively limited even the introduction of any pro-Black Democratic Party programs. While in retrospect, Roosevelt did not need the South to win in 1940 and 1944, his prospective judgment as the incumbent was not to alienate in any way what he felt might be needed support.

Shortly after World War II ended, the psychological impact of Nazi racism together with increasing militancy among Black and White civil rights forces brought the issue of racial equality to Roosevelt's successor, Harry Truman. Earlier, when a Missouri Senator, Truman had publicly stated his belief in legal equality, although he was not for ending all forms of segregation. It was not that Truman believed in social equality or in a complete abandonment of "separate but equal," but he was personally willing to commit his party to putting national racial laws on the books to control state administered inequities before the law.

When a fact-finding committee of Northerners and Southern liberals selected by the President—the Presidential Committee on Civil Rights—recommended national legislation to help the victims of segregation in America, the lines of racial battle began to be tightly drawn in the Democratic Party. Truman's subsequent mes-

16.   See Herbert Garfinkel, *When Negroes March: The March on Washington Movement in the Organizational Politics for FEPC* (Glencoe, Illinois: Free Press, 1959), pp. 37–61.

sage to Congress in 1948 did not include the Committee's call for an end to segregation but did propose the following landmark policy changes: a Federal Fair Employment Practices Act (to replace the wartime FEPC); strong anti-lynching laws, and the protection of Negro voting rights.[17]

This racial program brought forth vehement protest from the South, but it also demonstrated in the counter-responses of Northerners the new strategic approaches among Northern urban politicians and important presidential advisers. Formulations of new and different political strategies were offered to a President who felt he could ignore the outrage of the South. James Sundquist described the political reactions of Truman's inner core of advisers:

> The professional politicians in the Truman circle instinctively recoiled. The cabinet was split. But Truman's principal planner of political strategy for the 1948 campaign was Clark M. Clifford, his special counsel, and Clifford had just written a brief for boldness. Negroes might hold the balance of power in several large Northern states, wrote Clifford. "The Negro voter has become a cynical, hard-boiled trader," and the Republicans were bidding high. Besides, Clifford argued, "as always, the South can be considered safely Democratic. And in formulating national policy, it can be safely ignored."[18]

Thus Truman and Clifford were gambling on the new dynamics of race that recognized the growing importance of Blacks in key states of the Northern urban coalition and at the same time believing, erroneously, that the introduction of racial issues would not cause significant defections among Southerners in the general election.

In Truman's racial proposals for national Democratic policy, the new strategic dynamics of the party in "post-rule" nomination politics can be seen. By 1948 Truman no longer had great popular support in the Democratic electorate, and it is reasonable to assume that he would not have risked his chances for renomination if the

---

17. James L. Sundquist, *Dynamics of the Party System: Alignment and Realignment of Political Parties in the United States* (Washington, D.C.: Brookings Institution, 1973), p. 248.
18. *Ibid.*, pp. 247–48.

segregation forces within the party had had the strategic benefits of the two-thirds rule. Truman's security in his power to gain the party's nomination reflected not only the changing power of the different factions uneasily held within the Democratic Party, but it also demonstrated the inability of one faction to thwart a coalition of other important factions as it had in the past. New strategic realities, both internal and external to the new Democratic Party, were already part of political calculations.

The counter-response to Truman's injection of race in national Democratic Party politics followed almost immediately. Only a few days after Truman articulated his position in his January 1948 State of the Union message, a group of Southern governors met in Florida and threatened an immediate break with the national party, the establishment of a new conservative party, and opposition to Truman's re-election unless the President reversed himself on the racial commitments within forty days. Then in May 1948, upon failing to convince President Truman to change his mind, these governors met with other like-minded Southerners at a major pre-convention conclave attended by more than two thousand anti-civil rights Democrats in Mississippi, and the conclave passed resolutions for bolting the national party unless the civil rights policies were defeated and the old two-thirds rule was reinstated at the Democratic convention in July.[19]

Having stirred up the Southern Democrats to a fever pitch, Truman subsequently softened the White House draft of the Democratic Party's racial platform for the national convention. But since the ideological lines had already hardened, the convictions of many politicians both North and South were no longer able to be compromised. Young, liberal political aspirants such as Hubert Humphrey insisted on the stronger position of Truman's earlier proposals for inclusion in the Democratic Party platform of 1948, and, interestingly, these reformers were joined by many regular organization politicians, who were themselves worried about Black and

19.   Arthur M. Schlesinger, Jr., *History of United States Political Parties,* Vol. IV, 1945–1972 (New York: Chelsea House, 1973), p. 3316.

White civil rights defectors to Henry A. Wallace's left-wing campaign. Party "bosses" such as Bronx Democrat Ed Flynn, who were never known as passionate liberals on racial matters, joined the battle, with Flynn stating that a good civil rights fight was "what we need to stir up this Convention and win the election."[20]

Then at the convention the party "bosses" from the major Northern cities joined with White and Black racial liberals to beat down Southern amendments, and forced adoption of the Northern plank by a vote of 651-1/2 to 582-1/2—with Truman supporters voting against the South. Following the vote, almost half the Alabama delegates and all of the Mississippi delegates walked out of the convention, beginning Southern delegate conflict with the national party that continued for decades.

The result of the convention vote on this key racial plank was suggestive of the power of intimidation under the two-thirds rule on such crucial racial issues, for the South was able to piece together a minority that while short of the simple majority needed in 1948 was more than sufficient to stop Truman under the old rule. Thus even the racial input of the 1948 platform, modest by today's standards, would have most probably blocked any presidential nomination attempted under the old rules. Racial policy was increasingly becoming an internal Democratic Party issue after three-quarters of a century of suppression. Indeed, what was happening was that serious presidential candidates, present and future, had grasped the strategic political reality that espousal of strong civil rights positions would not automatically end any hopes they might have for the Democratic presidential nomination.

Race as a matter of national Democratic Party policy had, therefore, been set in motion at the presidential level, but because key Southern Democrats and their conservative Republican allies maintained congressional control over major legislation, the thrust for racial progress was to remain largely administrative. Lacking legislative support, many presidential positions taken by Truman

20.   Irwin Ross, *The Loneliest Campaign: The Truman Victory of 1948* (New York: New American Library, 1968), p. 125.

were largely symbolic in nature, although some dramatic executive implementation was effected, e.g., the Executive Order issued by Truman integrating the armed forces in 1948. In terms of major policy breakthroughs on race, however, little could be accomplished in Truman's war-beleaguered second administration, as both his declining popular and congressional support further curtailed his racial policy initiatives.

In fact, the next major challenge to continuing resistance against changing the racial status quo was generated, instead, from outside of party politics through the 1954 Supreme Court *Brown* decision outlawing segregation, a decision that forced new racial issues of implementation into national party politics. The South's inability to deal legally with race on a "separate but equal" basis after this decision triggered a great number of new political dynamics that have had much to do with changing the shape of the political alignments in present-day politics.

RACE AND A RESPONDING ELECTORATE

The initial conflict that followed the *Brown* decision occurred during the second Eisenhower administration, a circumstance that offered a short-term political respite for the Democrats with respect to political losses over racial issues, since the first actual confrontations of court implementation (including the use of Federal troops) were to come during a Republican administration. Because of Eisenhower's executive action to enforce desegregation, reluctant as it was,[21] the racial backlash to the *Brown* decision fell disproportionately on the Republican incumbent rather than on the Northern leadership of the Democratic Party which had openly welcomed the decision. As a matter of fact, the inability of the electorate to perceive the political implication immediately in party terms is suggested in the presidential returns of the 1956 Republi-

21. Eisenhower never praised or endorsed the *Brown* decision, but merely accepted it.

can landslide: seven Southern states, mostly from the Deep South, voted for Democrat Adlai Stevenson, and three of these states, ironically, were states that had defected to the states' rights candidate, Strom Thurmond, back in 1948.

Some of the uncertainty in the electorate was due to the position on racial matters that Stevenson took in the campaign, for Stevenson sought to moderate earlier Democratic divisions on civil rights by urging the nation to move slowly on the integrating of races—despite more aggressive statements in his party's platform. Rights could not be achieved by troops or bayonets, Stevenson believed: "We must" he asserted, "proceed gradually, not upsetting habits or traditions that are older than the Republic."[22]

The hostile political reaction of White Southerners was limited for the first year or two of the subsequent Kennedy administration. Although Kennedy had taken clear-cut positions in his acceptance speech at the 1960 convention and later in his inaugural speech, he generally maintained a rather low profile on the racial issue during the first Federal-state confrontations early in his administration, generally relying on Federal marshals rather than on Federal troops.[23] But after troops finally became necessary to ensure admittance of Black students to the University of Mississippi and the University of Alabama, the moderately pro-Kennedy and pro-Democratic sentiment in the South was rapidly and dramatically transformed. Lubell's detailed surveys of this period found that Federal implementation of the law between 1961 and 1963 had stirred bitter anger against Kennedy and the Democratic administration on racial grounds, so much so that large numbers of Southerners vowed to support either the Republican nominee or the rebellious Governor George Wallace in the presidential election of 1964.[24]

22. Schlesinger, *op. cit.*, p. 2698.
23. For an account of Kennedy's initial emphasis on executive rather than legislative pressure, see Charles V. Hamilton, *The Bench and the Ballot: Southern Federal Judges and Black Voters* (New York: Oxford University Press, 1973), pp. 79–87.
24. See Lubell, *White and Black,* p. 117.

This growing disaffection in the South because of the identification of the Democratic Party with increasing racial change was more than just a momentary reaction to the use of troops to compel integration. For even in the face of the Johnson landslide of 1964, the states of the Deep South returned large majorities for Barry Goldwater. The emerging identification of the Democratic Party with racial change was clearly stated by Gerald Pomper in his analysis of both Northern and Southern attitudes:

> In 1956, there was no consensus of the parties' stand on the issues of school integration and fair employment. Differences between the parties were less likely to be seen, and Republicans were as likely as Democrats to be perceived as favoring federal action on civil rights. A startling reversal occurred in 1964; all partisan groups recognized the existence of the difference on this issue, and all were convinced that the Democrats stood more for government programs on behalf of Blacks.[25]

There seems to be no doubt that the positions of the candidates of the two major parties in that period, Lyndon Johnson and Barry Goldwater, highlighted and deepened the polarization between the parties on racial issues. On one hand Johnson had strongly committed himself to the civil rights proposals left in the wake of Kennedy's assassination, and pushed through the 1964 Civil Rights Act—legislation of historic importance. On the other hand, his opponent, Barry Goldwater, had taken a position squarely in opposition to Federal pressures against state rights in racial matters and had voted *against* the 1964 Civil Rights Act. He was, in fact, the first (but not the last) Republican to adopt a public "Southern strategy," running his 1964 campaign in sharply drawn ideological opposition to the Democratic administration's civil rights policies, although without racist demagoguery.

In the North, however, the situation was different. The polarizing force of racial backlash was also developing among Demo-

25. Gerald Pomper, "From Confusion to Clarity: Issues and American Voters, 1956–1968," *The American Political Science Review,* 66, 2 (June 1972), 420.

crats in 1964, evidenced by the unexpected strength shown by George Wallace in the 1964 primaries in Wisconsin, Indiana, and Maryland, where he gained between 25 to 43 percent of the vote. However, fears that Goldwater would dismantle valued social welfare programs, together with anxiety over his international adventurism, substantially offset the rising urban backlash among Whites in the North over racial change. It was not until the middle and late 1960s that the racial explosions in the cities and rising Black militancy finally activated major defections among Democrats. What was needed to produce actual electoral defections from traditional urban Democrats was a political "detonator," in Burnham's terms, that would enlarge racial fears and concerns to a point where they would override the normal Democratic advantage on other socio-economic issues—and this detonator was provided by the massive racial upheavals in the Northern cities between 1964 and 1968.

Riots and racial violence, conflict involving control of schools and community resources, and White fears of the breakdown of "law and order" during the period 1964-68 produced a fierce counterreaction among those less mobile Whites in the major cities. As Lubell and others have documented, a significant percentage of these urban Whites perceived racial violence, fear for one's personal safety, residential encroachment, and school busing problems as the responsibility of Democratic national policy.[26] And Lyndon Johnson as the visible champion of Black advancement clearly drew the focus of the racial backlash to his presidency.

Scammon and Wattenberg showed that, as early as 1965, President Johnson was already seen as pushing integration too fast by almost half the American population, and by September 1966 public opinion polls for the first time showed that a majority *in the North* believed that the administration was pushing integration too fast.[27] Still to follow were many presidentially designed, Black-

---

26.   See Lubell, *The Hidden Crisis,* pp. 97–113.
27.   Richard M. Scammon and Ben J. Wattenberg, *The Real Majority* (New York: Coward-McCann, 1970), p. 116.

identified programs and more exploding racial upheavals in the cities of the North. Johnson, to a far greater extent than Kennedy, had chosen to align his party clearly with the Northern polar forces on race.

The growing backlash in the Northern cities to Johnson's polar position was further extended by its incorporation into the issue of "law and order" (or even more broadly into the "social issue")—all of which were intermeshed with attitudes relating to a major decline in stability and safety in American cities. While racial issues and issues of law and order can in fact be distinguished from each other, many Whites seemed unable to do so. As perceived by many Whites, crime was disproportionately Black, terrifying riots were Black, and Black militants were everywhere on television threatening more destruction if demands were not met. Blacks and their "allies" in the Democratic administration were perceived as being against segregation, against the old status quo and, correspondingly, *for* change that was destructive and often violent. Those who opposed the administration were quick to take advantage of the cloudy distinctions between the issues of law and order and race.

As Sundquist pointed out, "Law and order was a *separable* issue from race, but it was not always a *separated* issue" in the eyes of many voters in the center of the storm.[28] The line between condoning violence and being unable to stop it was seemingly a difficult one to draw for the Johnson administration, and the linkage of disruption, crime, race, and a Democratic administration offered an excellent opportunity for Republican leaders to exacerbate the growing racial tensions before the 1968 election. The then Republican House leader, Gerald R. Ford, blended crime and Black militancy in this manner:

> The war at home—the war against crime—is being lost. The Administration appears to be in full retreat. The homes and the streets of America are no longer safe for our people. . . .

28. Sundquist, *Dynamics of the Party System,* p. 323.

When a Rap Brown and a Stokley Carmichael are allowed to run loose, to threaten law-abiding Americans with injury and death, it's time to slam the door on them and any like them—and slam it hard![29]

The impact of racial conflict as a mass issue working against the Democratic candidate can be seen in Table 15, where conservative racial attitudes are clearly linked to Nixon or Wallace votes and, conversely, liberal racial attitudes linked to votes for Democrat Humphrey in both these pivotal Northern regions. Indications of the forceful racial backlash among Whites can also be seen in the combined defections to Nixon and Wallace from racially conservative Democrats in both regions (25% in the Midwest and 19% in the East) compared to lesser defections among racially liberal Democrats (11% in the Midwest and 9% in the East). By 1968, in both these crucial regions of the North, racial conflict had made significant inroads among normally Democratic White voters.[30]

Although these data do not define voters by residential characteristics, other data indicate that the heaviest defections within these regions were in the major cities containing substantial Black populations. Lubell specifically identified the shrinking margins for the Democratic presidential candidate in 1968 after examining White urban districts on the cutting edge of racial conflict and finding a major shift to Wallace and Nixon among these traditional Democratic voters. After checking the precincts of major cities which showed racially motivated defections (a Wallace vote in excess of 25%), Lubell described the local situation in traditional Democratic strongholds in this manner:

29. *Ibid.*, pp. 325–26.
30. Whereas party/race defections offer no major regional surprises, interestingly it is among the increasing numbers of self-declared Independents that regional differences appear most pronounced, suggesting that there are different types of Independents along racial/regional lines. Inpendent racial conservatives, for example, voted heavily against the Democratic candidate, Hubert Humphrey, in the Midwest, while Independent racial conservatives in the East split their vote almost evenly.

TABLE 15. 1968 Presidential Vote by Region[a], Party Identification, and White Racial Attitudes

1968 Vote:	Humphrey	Nixon	Wallace	(Sample Sizes)
Midwest				
Racial Liberals[b]	*51%*	*45%*	*4%*	*(133)*
Democrats	86	14	–	(58)
Republicans	8	88	4	(33)
Independents	33	57	10	(42)
Racial Conservatives	*35*	*54*	*11*	*(191)*
Democrats	70	18	12	(76)
Republicans	5	89	6	(66)
Independents	18	62	20	(49)
East				
Racial Liberals	*60%*	*38%*	*2%*	*(137)*
Democrats	89	11	–	(66)
Republicans	17	83	–	(35)
Independents	51	46	3	(36)
Racial Conservatives	*36*	*56*	*8*	*(122)*
Democrats	74	19	7	(41)
Republicans	2	94	4	(49)
Independents	40	44	16	(32)

Source: Data from Survey Research Center, 1968

[a] Regions are those defined by the U.S. Census Bureau.

[b] Liberals are those giving answers deemed responsive to Black interests. See Appendix B, note 9 for scaling method.

Visiting these precincts was like inspecting a stretched-out warfront. Each Wallace precinct was like another outpost marking the borders to which Negro residential movement had pushed. On some streets the families who had voted for Wallace in 1968 were already gone, the area having turned entirely Black by 1969. Other streets simmered with the strains of neighborhood transition. At still other points, the Whites had drawn an unyielding line that permitted no Blacks to pass.[31]

Whereas local ethnic and racial conflicts in the past had tended to be suppressed in presidential elections, the heavy urban defections in the 1968 election indicated an increasing disposition among local White voters to blame racially connected problems on the leaders of the national Democratic Party, particularly the presidential candidate. The responsibility for the growing conflict between urban working-class Whites and Blacks was directed, not illogically, at the party in control of the national administration, one whose former leader, Lyndon Johnson, had firmly tied himself and his party to Black progress, and intoned on national television the symbolic refrain of Black aspiration, "We shall overcome."[32]

By 1968 racial conflict had cut deeply across traditionally Democratic urban groups and consequently the national Democratic Party, and though the activists in American politics were divided most deeply over Vietnam War policy, rank and file voters in the major cities of the urban belt were polarizing more over conflicts of race. As the reins maintaining old racial relationships were loosened, the force built by centuries of racial suppression exploded in American politics. For the Democrats—the apparent sponsors of the change in the status quo—the political price was high.

BLACK ELITES AND BLACK PARTY POWER

In tracing the widening force of race as an issue in the Democratic Party, one noteworthy factor remains to be analyzed, namely, the impact of Black party leadership on Democratic decisions. Most, if

31. Samuel Lubell, *The Hidden Crisis,* p. 105.
32. For an excellent overall assessment of race, Wallace, and presidential voting in 1968, see Philip E. Converse, Warren E. Miller, Jerrold G. Rusk, and Arthur C. Wolfe, "Continuity and Change in American Politics: Parties and Issues in the 1968 Election," *American Political Science Review,* 63 (December 1969), 1083–1105.

not all, national Democratic deliberations on racial matters have, until recently, involved conflict among Whites *about* Blacks, with Black elites playing a minuscule role in direct party bargaining. Not without reason, of course, because Black leaders traditionally saw little hope of any significant gains that could be made through regular party machinery that had consistently suppressed racial issues.

The impact that elites may have in determining presidential leadership can be, as we have seen, a decisive element in structuring party policy. However, the ability of elites to shape the direction of the party ordinarily depends in substantial measure on their manipulative and mobilizing skills, which, when properly applied, can bring about disproportionate gains for one interest or another. For Whites, the party system, attracting the principal political leadership cadres, has been the prime arena of political conflict from early in the country's history. But with respect to the development of Black political elites, the situation has been entirely different, for the suppression of race as a national party issue since the end of Reconstruction essentially closed that avenue of politics for Black leadership elites.[33] With few exceptions, Black political leaders have had to focus their energies in the past primarily on the courts and administrative agencies for political and social gains, playing only a limited role in the lower levels of local party politics in the North.[34] Until the 1960s party politics was simply not a valued arena of conflict for Black political activists, since other avenues of politics offered greater promise of reward.

In 1954, the *Brown* decision gave new scope to racial conflict and opened additional non-party avenues of expression for Black political elites—in the courts and in the streets. In the South this generated a new group of Black political elites, whose "protest

---

33. C. Vann Woodward, *Reunion and Reaction: The Compromise of 1877 and the End of Reconstruction* (Boston: Little, Brown, 1966), pp. 226–29.
34. James Q. Wilson, *Negro Politics: The Search for Leadership* (New York: Free Press, 1960), pp. 71–76.

politics" leadership helped change the face of the South in less than a decade. In the North, the dynamics unleashed by the protest movement combined with other explosive elements in ghetto life and brought forth a different kind of Black street leader—less "non-violent" than his Southern counterpart in style and not seeking equal rights as much as a larger piece of the political and economic pie.

The shift of focus from legal rights to tangible economic and political benefits also changed the arena of conflict from primarily *non-party* to *party* politics. The courts and the streets could provide gains, but with major limitations of scope. And as Black elites turned to party politics, certain leadership problems emerged—difficulties stemming primarily from successful Black leadership styles used earlier outside the constraints of the party system. Although non-violent "protest politics" in the South and "street politics" in the North differed in their short-run objectives and methods, both nevertheless produced leaders whose political style dealt in generally indivisible and symbolic terms such as "rights," "justice," and "control"—and relied upon the charismatic, spontaneous, and oratorical qualities of their leaders to gain primarily "nonnegotiable demands." Whether it was Martin Luther King, Jr.'s march to Selma for political equality, school boycotts, or welfare sit-ins, the style of these leaders presented political demands in essentially symbolic form, seeking to dramatize the issues in moral and indivisible terms.

The application of this type of leadership in the 1970s, however, seems to be sharply limited, and the question remains whether a style of Black leadership, shaped primarily by the political needs of the 1950s and 1960s, can be rechanneled to meet the new demands of party-oriented conflict. For example, certain aspects of this anti-brokerage "movement" leadership were manifested in the efforts of the Mississippi Freedom Democratic Party (MFDP) at the 1964 Democratic convention to gain major procedural reforms that included the unseating of the regular Mississippi delegation—a delegation chosen by local (and racist) procedures. The compro-

mise worked out by the Johnson/Humphrey forces, while not allowing the seating of the MFDP delegation (two members were to
be seated as delegates-at-large), did provide for a mandatory loyalty oath by state delegates to the national ticket and, most importantly, included agreement that a new national party rule prohibit-
ing discrimination would be enforced at the 1968 convention.
However, despite the significant changes agreed to by the national
leadership, the compromise—though sufficient to lead to the de-
parture of all but four Mississippi regulars—was rejected by the
MFDP leadership as the brokerage work of "bankrupt liberals"
and had to be accepted by the convention without the agreement
and in the absence of the MFDP.[35]

While it may be too early to judge the full implications of the
1972 Democratic convention, the convention that year was the
first with a significant potential Black input and reflected in several
ways the very problems of Black leadership in adapting to the new
requirements of party-oriented conflict. New procedures stemming
from the 1964 and 1968 conventions together with the new reforms
developed by the McGovern-Fraser committee opened the 1972
convention to major increases in Black participation, so that Black
delegates were sufficient numerically (483 out of 3203 delegates)[36]
to play more than just a symbolic role, as in prior conventions. Indeed, it was not the lack of a sizable convention delegation or the
lack of participation in the manifest business of the convention
that was most notable, but rather the presence of symbolic representation *without* Blacks playing a direct and vital role in the primary function of the convention—nominating a presidential candidate. If anything, the public view of the convention activities (i.e.,

35. Jack Minnis, "The Mississippi Freedom Democratic Party: A New
     Declaration of Independence," *Freedom Ways,* Vol. 5, No. 2 (Spring
     1965), 270–72. For another perspective on the MFDP at the 1964 con-
     vention, see Stokley Carmichael and Charles V. Hamilton, *Black Power,
     Politics of Liberation in America* (New York: Random House, 1967),
     pp. 86–97.
36. The Democratic National Committee, *Congressional Quarterly Weekly
     Supplement,* Vol. XXX, No. 28 (July 8, 1972), 1642.

the numbers of speakers on the floor, in committee, and on the dais) suggested a far greater political input from Blacks than was actually made in power terms.

This lack of vital input in the candidate selection process was evidenced by the fact that a month after the crucial California victory of George McGovern, Black elites were still debating about whether to push McGovern symbolically "over the top," having failed to develop any cohesive party strategy in the months before the final primaries in California and New York—contests that for all practical purposes sealed the nomination or at least limited the viability of all the candidates except McGovern.[37] Black delegates and leaders themselves were almost unanimous in their publicly proclaimed disappointment at the disharmony and diffuseness of Black input at the convention, some citing the discordant activities of various leaders for the lack of cohesiveness among Black elites.[38]

Black leaders supporting George McGovern, such as Georgia State Representative Julian Bond, were critical of the Congressional Black Caucus's refusal to endorse McGovern until he had publicly endorsed a "Black Bill of Rights," with Bond stating that "most of the [Black] Southerners I've talked to don't want the [Congressional Black] Caucus negotiating for them."[39] Others, such as Jesse Jackson, felt that Black Representative Shirley Chisholm's presidential candidacy had effectively blocked the selection

37. Jay M. Schwamm, Humphrey's campaign chairman in New York, conceded that not preparing a slate in New York turned out to have been a major Humphrey miscalculation primarily due to limited campaign resources, one that, in effect, made California the decisive primary. McGovern's narrow victory in California (which was considered a stronger McGovern state than New York) could not be tested again in New York because Humphrey's forces had gambled that other slates, such as Senator Muskie's, would be easily available to their candidate—and they were not. Interview with Jay M. Schwamm, New York City, June 10, 1972.

38. Paul Delaney, *New York Times,* July 16, 1972, p. 42; from another perspective, this same view of Black disunity was found by Imamu Amiri Baraka, "Toward the Creation of Institutions for All African People," *Black World,* XXI, 12 (October 1972) 54–78.

39. Delaney, *New York Times,* June 2, 1972, 44.

of a male leader behind whom all Blacks could rally, and that in the absence of a suitable Black presidential candidate, the battle among Black elites revolved largely around age—younger Blacks like himself, Coretta King, and Julian Bond for McGovern, and older party politicians and labor leaders of the "old guard" for Hubert Humphrey.[40]

In any case, the lack of cohesion in Black political strategy limited any thrust by Black leaders to affect the selection of the presidential candidate significantly; and much of the efforts of the Black elites, such as the Black Congressional Caucus, were spent on secondary aspects of the convention, such as planks in the platform and seeking convention acceptance of a "non-negotiable Black Bill of Rights" that included a $6500 minimum income.[41] The conflict among Black leaders also indicated, at least in part, that the personal qualities so beneficial to non-party political leadership—charismatic, symbolic, and rhetorical—had to be welded to those other needed organizational, manipulative, and strategic talents required in party politics.

However, while conflicts between different Black elites were in part responsible for the limited group role at the Democratic convention, there is evidence to suggest that the indecisive voting behavior of Blacks in the electorate at large also contributed to this ineffectiveness by offering little direction to Black leaders. After clearly rejecting Shirley Chisholm's presidential campaign,[42] the Black primary voter gave indecisive and hesitant responses to both the principal contenders, Hubert Humphrey and George McGovern, and consequently gave no focusing signals to Black party elites. Surveys of Black primary voters found that McGovern got 15 percent of the Black vote in Wisconsin, 10 percent of the Black

40. Delaney, *New York Times,* July 16, 1972, 42.
41. Delaney, *New York Times,* June 2, 1972, 22.
42. Representative Shirley Chisholm's primary campaign garnered total votes of only 3.6 percent in Florida, 2.8 percent in Michigan, 2.7 percent in Maryland and 4.6 percent in California. According to CBS News' California Primary Survey, she received only 17 percent of the Black vote in California.

vote in Pennsylvania, 35 percent in Massachusetts, and 25 percent in Michigan before finally gaining about 50 percent of the vote in California. Hubert Humphrey, on the other hand, started with strong Black support, gaining 75 percent of the Black vote in the multi-candidate Wisconsin race, about 65 percent of the Black vote in Michigan and Ohio, before finally finishing with less than 50 percent of the vote in the California primary.[43]

The Black vote in the primaries was, in fact, less focused at the end of the campaign than it was at the beginning, and for our analysis of intra-party conflict, this reluctance to support either candidate with strength is of major significance. In essence the inability of McGovern or Humphrey to gain the solid support of Black voters indicated a certain ambivalence among Blacks in the electorate toward the core support behind both candidates, the labor/organization interests behind Hubert Humphrey, and the New Politics interests behind George McGovern. Whereas the New Politics orientation on symbolic positions may have enabled McGovern to secure greater support from Black political elites,[44] similar confidence in McGovern's candidacy was not found in the Black electorate at large. The Black voter was, in effect, offered two presidential candidates, each broadly representing one of two important wings of White conflict in the party (the Wallace wing was obviously unacceptable), and neither of the candidates of these two factions emerged as a clear choice of the Black electorate.

Militating against the shift to McGovern in the Black electorate was the fact that Hubert Humphrey's personal support for Black causes had been established as far back as the 1948 convention. But in addition, analysis of Black voting behavior suggests other reasons that might also help account for the half-hearted

43. Yankelovich Survey, *New York Times,* June 9, 1972, 1. Also, CBS News, California Primary Survey.
44. The sponsorship of the National Welfare Rights Bill by McGovern proposing a minimum income of $6500 was only a symbolic gesture, but as such it was representative of the political style of McGovern's campaign.

embrace of such a racially responsive candidate as George McGovern, reasons related to the group basis of McGovern support as well as his own personal campaign style. As indicated earlier, McGovern's intra-party support was anchored among affluent suburbanites, anti-war activists, intellectuals, and young supporters, all primarily from the middle class, and far removed socially and economically from the primarily working-class Black voter. Although Black elites themselves moved easily among the New Politics activists, there may well have been a certain working-class suspicion among Blacks at large of a movement so basically middle class in style and so detached from "bread and butter" concerns. Indeed, the evidence of past political research indicates that the ideological, moral, and "public interest" approach to politics of McGovern's campaign would be unlikely to appeal deeply to any working-class voter either White or Black.[45]

It may well be that Black voters, despite McGovern's stronger racial position, did not respond to McGovern because of the highly ideological nature of his campaign, since, as Gerhard Lenski has shown, most Blacks do not perceive politics in the same way as the college-educated and the affluent. Rather, Black workers respond to political life less systematically, less idealistically, and more self-interestedly—just as White working-class people do.[46] Therefore, McGovern's ideologically focused candidacy, stressing complex ideas, cultural principles, and a heavy emphasis on the "public interest," together with his unappealing personal campaign style, may well have struck a peculiar chord with Blacks.

However, although sharing many common economic and social needs with the White working class, Black identification with the labor/organization wing of the Democratic Party nevertheless

45. See James Q. Wilson, *The Amateur Democrat, op. cit.* pp. 258–88; also see James Q. Wilson and Edward C. Banfield, "Public Regardingness as a Value Premise in Voting Behavior," *American Political Science Review,* 58 (December 1964), 876–87; and James Q. Wilson and Edward C. Banfield, "Political Ethos Revisited," *American Political Science Review,* 64 (December 1971), 1048–62.
46. Lenski, *The Religious Factor,* p. 160.

brought special tensions as well. Some of labor's leadership and many of the remaining regular organization politicians have historically resisted Black advances, not simply on the basis of their own personal bias, but as a result of pressure from their constituents, the White working class and urban ethnic groups. As a result, conflict stimulated by the large migrations of Black population into White areas has seemingly presented social, economic, and political progress for Blacks as a closed socio-political process, i.e., gains for one group come at the direct expense of the other. In consequence, even among the traditionally liberal United Auto Workers—whose leadership has been long identified with the Democratic liberal wing—George Wallace's Michigan primary campaign gained the vote of over one-half of the White UAW membership, primarily because of race-related issues.[47] Thus at present the racial antagonisms between a substantial portion of Black and White workers seem to have cut across common class interests, putting a Black political alliance with labor under different but nevertheless persistent tension as well.

The entrance of Black political elites into party politics comes at a critical point for the Democratic Party, for as the last two conventions have demonstrated, neither of the two viable core factions, the labor/organization wing and the New Politics wing, can dominate the other without losing large numbers of voters and, consequently, the presidency. Ironically, Black political leadership in the Democratic Party may well become a crucial factor in determining what kind of candidate the Democratic Party will offer to the American electorate in the future, for the almost exclusive concentration of Blacks among Democrats provides a potential intra-party constituency of approximately 20 percent—and, if sufficiently mobilized, may become a pivotal influence in intra-party conflict.

Possibly more than any other group in the Democratic coalition, Blacks stand to lose the most with the defeat of the Demo-

47.   Yankelovich Survey, *New York Times,* May 18, 1972, p. 18.

cratic presidential candidate, for their principal governmental gains outside of court action have come primarily through the initiative and instrumentality of the Executive Office—specifically post-World War II Democratic Presidents.[48] Any reasonable comparison of the Kennedy-Johnson presidencies and the Nixon-Ford presidencies demonstrates that Democratic Presidents are decisively more responsive to Black interests, and that Black political leverage on a Republican President is negligible. Exhortations by Black leaders to exert power in both parties do not take into account the fact that the strongest core of Republican presidential voters is now in the South, and, as party divisions over racial issues in the North now stand, Democrats are far more racially liberal than Republicans (see Table 15). Thus the continuance of at least a modified "Southern strategy" by the Republicans is likely, which effectively limits the ability of Blacks to utilize both parties for their presidential political interests.

Lacking a genuine two-party alternative, it is therefore of crucial concern to Blacks that the internal factionalism that has divided the party be somehow ameliorated so that Democratic presidential influence over both bureaucratic implementation of existing law as well as over new race policy initiatives may be regained. Thus a pivotal question facing Blacks within the party is whether they can help reforge a majority coalition by helping to bring about the nomination of a candidate who is able to reconcile party factions and win the votes of the electorate at large; a strategy, it appears, that would now require Black elites pressing the party away from overly ideological politics—i.e., away from supporting candidates like McCarthy and McGovern of the New Politics wing—and toward a more traditional candidate stressing the accommodation of various interests and the personal element in politics.

48. See James L. Sundquist, *Politics and Policy: The Eisenhower, Kennedy and Johnson Years* (Washington, D.C.: Brookings Institution, 1968), pp. 221–86. See also Ronald C. Moe and Steven C. Teel, "Congress as Policy-Maker: A Necessary Reappraisal," *Political Science Quarterly,* 85 (September 1970), 461–62.

Of course, this kind of strategy also produces other coalitional tensions for Black party elites in terms of their past intra-party alliances, since successful efforts by Black elites to increase Black participation at the Democratic conventions have come primarily through Black elite alliances with the anti-war, reform wing of the party. For example, in the procedural challenge of the regular Mississippi state delegation by the Mississippi Freedom Democrats in 1964, in the struggle against Lester Maddox's Georgia delegation by Julian Bond's Loyal National Democrats in 1968, and in subsequent delegate reforms in 1972 and 1974, Black party activists have made consistent and successful intra-party alliances with their most sympathetic audience, the liberal reform wing of the Party, on "loaded" procedural issues before the convention.

However, the Black alliance with reform interests, though effective in the short run (it successfully won a last-minute change in the "affirmative action" language at the 1974 mini-convention), does not promise as much solidity over the long term. Unlike New Politics interests, Black elites have exhibited little commitment to primary elections, intra-party democracy, or procedural reform as an ideal; rather, procedural changes such as mandatory quotas of representation have been viewed as a means of "getting in the game" by whatever means is feasible. Whereas the middle-class New Politics faction of the party gains philosophical satisfaction and strategic advantage by opening the party to mass democratic competition, the same is not the case for Blacks. How the game is played means little to a group whose political idealism has been tempered by harsh experience; rather, the end result of substantial Black representation has been the essential objective of Black elites in intra-party politics. Substance, in this case, clearly dominates form.

But the weakest link in any future alliance of Blacks and New Politics Whites lies in the ability of White reformers to press their principles to the point of accepting defeat in the general election as a price of conscience. For Black elites, the relatively unprotected socio-economic position of the Black rank and file (compared with that of their relatively affluent allies) makes defeat in the post-nomination election far less acceptable even in the short run. Therefore, though Black elites require New Politics elements as allies in gaining and holding procedural reforms favorable to elite representation (e.g., the Women's Caucus was a crucial elite ally of Blacks at the 1974 mini-convention), they cannot as easily afford stressing principles at the price of rejection in the subsequent general election. The tentative economic position of Black masses in America places specific limits on Black alliances of principle that threaten rank and file gains needed in the immediate future.

Because of these unique circumstances it falls upon emergent Black party elites to play a very difficult role in future intra-party Democratic politics—in effect, trying to limit the destructive aftermath of internal cleavages on the election possibilities of the eventual Democratic candidate. To be successful in this new role, more private bargaining with the candidate and other competing interests will most likely have to replace public demands that appear "non-negotiable"; and new style "grass-roots" Black leaders will have to extend their base of mass support among Blacks to the national level, so as to enable them to fulfill the strategic demands of this new focus of Black politics in the party system.

Whether Black elites and their supporters in the mass electorate can successfully play such a difficult role in the presidential selection process is for the future of American politics finally to determine. But just the fact that Blacks could have such a vital impact on the nomination and election of a Democratic Party presidential candidate is indicative of the tremendous changes in race/ party relationships that have come about in just the last several decades. In fact, in little more than four decades, the Democratic Party has moved in stages from a national party firmly supporting racial suppression, to one broadly advocating the rights and interests of Black Americans, to the party of today where Black internal power is developing an independent base of its own that may become a pivotal force in future party politics.

In the perspective of the past four decades, the introduction of race into national Democratic deliberations can be seen to be critically related to the breaking of a crucial institutional lock on the expansion of intra-party conflict—the two-thirds rule—a rule that had effectively denied racial options to aspiring Democratic presidential candidates and, in consequence, limited the development of presidential racial policies. The rule change was, in effect, both a party response to elite demands for a more effective presidential selection process, and, after its removal, a powerful stimulus for new racial demands on the national party. Party elites, responding to national concerns that were essentially non-racial in origin, had formulated new "rules of the game" for gaining the prize of the presidential nomination, and, as a crucial institutional constraint was removed from national party choices, the party and the party system were further opened to the dynamics of racial conflict.

Over time the Democratic "Sun" party has become the party of inclusion rather than exclusion, seeking simultaneously to house the traditional White urban working-class, along with new middle-class suburban groups, new issue publics, and, most importantly, emergent Black interests—groups perhaps too disparate for one party to encompass successfully. The expansion of racial conflict in particular has both brought progress for Blacks and, temporarily at least, weakened the White urban underpinnings of the traditional coalition as well—a circumstance most clearly manifested in the power of the Wallace movement in the urban North.

The dilemma facing both Black interests and the Democratic Party is that as the party has actually attempted to deal with long-suppressed issues of race—with some successes and some failures—the presidential party has become firmly identified with much of the instability that is the natural after-effect of long delayed changes in the racial status quo. As the advocate of change, the national Democrat leadership has felt the electoral impact of racial backlash, first in the South and then in Northern strongholds, a reaction that has added immeasurably to the problem of remaining the majority party. The unwillingness of the modern Republican Party to press for racial progress has made the Democratic Party, in effect, the racial battleground of American politics, seriously threatening the majority coalition's internal stability.

New political demands are thus being made on a party system that has historically either shunned efforts to resolve major racial divisions or, as in the case of the Civil War, failed outright, and serious doubts must remain as to whether the Democratic Party can successfully manage conflict of such divisive intensity. The nationalizing of the Democratic Party from its sectional base was a necessary step in enlarging the scope of racial conflict in the party system, but the enormous expansion of racial conflict has, in turn, badly weakened the Democratic Party as an effective electoral vehicle for gaining presidential power and lessened the chances for further racial progress.

III

The
Democratic Party
and the
Party System

7

Candidacy and the Changing Shape of Conflict

Many scholars of American politics have pointed to the substantial lack of participation by Americans as a limiting factor in the development of a genuine democracy. Schattschneider postulated, for example, that the "socialization of conflict," i.e., extending the scope of political conflict to include more of the unrepresented public, was essential to the democratic process, and only through such broad public involvement in election choices of competing leaders and organizations could the public effectively participate in the decision-making process of government.[1] Participation by the public in electoral conflict was the "democratic" answer, Schattschneider felt, to the disproportionate power of pressure groups and advantaged socio-economic elites in American political life.

In a provocative analysis of American parties and voter turnout, Burnham traced the actual erosion of, rather than an increase in, this much needed participation by the mass public in party competition, noting that the link between the mass of voters and the government had been weakening:

1. E. E. Schattschneider, *The Semi-Sovereign People,* p. 141.

In the United States these transformations over the past century have involved devolution, a dissociation from politics among a growing segment of the eligible electorate and an apparent deterioration of the bonds of party linkage between electorate and government. . . . Such a pattern of development is pronouncedly retrograde compared with those which have obtained elsewhere in the Western world during the past century.[2]

Burnham found that the peak of voter turnout in presidential elections of approximately 80 percent of all eligible voters was registered between 1876 and 1896—including the newly enfranchised Negro voters—and has not been closely approached since that time. Turnout subsequently declined to about 50 percent of eligible voters by the 1920s, before the nationalizing forces of economic crisis in the 1930s pushed the electoral participation of the public back to the low 60 percent levels, where it remained until 1960 with the exception of slight declines in 1944 and 1948.

Other scholars have questioned the validity of Burnham's analysis, citing for example the absence of voting restrictions such as registration requirements, the existence of vote selling, and a narrower range of eligible voters, as factors that could have abnormally swollen voting turnout in the nineteenth century.[3] But whether or not one fully accepts Burnham's historic comparison, or the explanations he advances for such erosion, the probability is that turnout has significantly diminished for a number of reasons since the nineteenth century and remains sluggish and unresponsive despite significant improvement in transportation, major innovations in communications, and substantial increases in education in the United States.

2. Walter Dean Burnham, "The Changing Shape of the American Political Universe," *American Political Science Review,* 59 (March 1965), 7.
3. See Philip E. Converse, "Change in the American Electorate," in *The Human Meaning of Social Change,* ed. Angus Campbell and Philip Converse (New York: Russell Sage Foundation, 1972), pp. 263–301. See also comments and rejoinders by Walter Dean Burnham, Jerrold G. Rusk, and Philip E. Converse in *American Political Science Review,* 68 (September 1974), 1002–57.

Participation in mass electoral conflict between the parties actually began to decline again from 1960 to 1972 despite the fact that this period contained an extraordinary amount of intense social and political conflict. Major changes in the status of Black Americans in the South in the early 1960s, acrimonious divisions over Vietnam war policy, university upheavals, and exploding riots in major Northern American cities did not seem to rouse the public to greater involvement in the electoral conflict between the two major parties. And claims to the effect that participation was low because the candidates were as politically similar as "Ike" and "Mike" lost much of their convincing force when participation dropped to an almost fifty-year low of 55 percent in the more ideologically perceived Nixon-McGovern campaign in 1972.[4]

Of critical interest for the present analysis is the fact that while the voting universe of the two-party system has clearly been contracting since 1960, the scope and intensity of participation *within* the individual party universe, i.e., intra-party mass conflict, has rapidly increased in this period—and of particular importance, the substantial increases in participation have been focused primarily within the Democratic Party.

In Table 16 we can see that when each party is examined separately, changes in the scope and intensity of *popular* conflict within each party are not at all similar. In terms of the number of very competitive presidential primary confrontations, the Democrats have outnumbered the Republicans 32 to 13 since 1948, with the greatest differences (22 to 6) occurring in the last four nomination races from 1960 to 1972. And in respect to rank and file participation in the nominating process, seriously contested primaries drew almost sixteen million Democrats and only about four million Republicans in the past four campaigns.[5]

4. See Arthur H. Miller, Warren E. Miller, Alden S. Raine, Thad A. Brown, "A Majority Party in Disarray: Policy Polarization in the 1972 Election." Center for Political Studies, University of Michigan. Paper presented at APSA Convention, New Orleans, 1973.
5. I am indebted to Ronald Susser for assistance in the preparation of Tables 16 and 17.

TABLE 16.   Presidential Primary Competition in Northern States
1948–1972[a]

	Number of Competitive Primaries[b]	Total Popular Vote In Competitive Primaries
Democrats		
* 1948	0	0
1952	4	809,000
1956	2	2,034,000
1960	2	676,000
* 1964	2	1,089,000
1968	6	4,566,000
1972	12	10,260,000
Republicans		
1948	3	671,000
1952	5	1,351,000
* 1956	0	0
1960	0	0
1964	6	3,972,000
1968	0	0
* 1972	0	0

[a] States with open primaries, i.e., no party registration restrictions, and states with non-preference delegate primaries are not included; votes are rounded to nearest thousand.

[b] A competitive primary is defined as one in which the winner received less than 65 percent of the total vote, and at least 10 percent of eligible voters turned out to vote.

* Denotes years in which party had incumbent President seeking re-election.

In these last four contests for the presidential nomination, each party has had an incumbent seeking re-election in only one year, the Democrats in 1964 (Johnson) and the Republicans in 1972 (Nixon); and yet the parties differed substantially in both the number of primaries that were seriously contested and the scope of rank and file participation. In fact, in two out of three of the races without a party incumbent, the Republicans had no seriously contested primaries at all (1960 and 1968).

The evidence of the last four presidential nominations clearly suggests the growing predilection of Democrats to utilize the primary election process as a method of candidate selection, as Democratic candidates and their elites seek to involve rank and file supporters in mass party decisions. For the Republicans, however, not only are truly competitive primaries less frequent, but rank and file sentiment when it is expressed does not appear to carry as much weight in Republican Party elite deliberations. For example, in the ideologically divisive 1964 Goldwater campaign, Goldwater gained the nomination after winning only one major contested preferential primary (California), and that with only 51 percent of the vote against Nelson Rockefeller. In two other direct primary contests he lost to Rockefeller in Oregon and to Lodge in New Hampshire.[6]

The growing tendency of Democrats to involve themselves in public conflict can also be seen in the relative turnout of party rank and file in states where party registration figures provide reliable estimates of primary participation, as shown in Table 17.

Although these selected states include the votes of non-contested as well as contested primaries, the distinction between the parties in terms of primary election conflict is clear, particularly in the intensely contested intra-party struggles of 1964, 1968, and 1972.[7] For example, the Republican turnout in 1964 was substantially less than that stimulated by the two hotly contested Democratic races in 1968 and 1972, and even in 1968, when there was no incumbent of either party running and Republican chances for victory were high, the Republican turnout in primary elections remained very low. The evidence points not only to a growing Dem-

6. Gerald Pomper, *Nominating the President: The Politics of Convention Choice* (New York: Norton, 1966), p. 272.
7. Using a different approach to measuring primary turnout (including only competitive primaries), William D. Morris and Otto A. Davis also found substantial differences between parties from 1964 to 1972. Paper delivered at the 1975 Annual Meeting of the American Political Science Association, Hilton Hotel, San Francisco, California, September 2–5, 1975.

TABLE 17.   Turnout Rate of Registered Voters in Presidential Preference Primaries in Selected States[a]

	% Democratic Turnout	% Republican Turnout
1948	27*	26
1952	33	51
1956	43	41*
1960	38	44
1964	38*	45
1968	51	34
1972	67	43*

[a] States are those that maintain registration records of both parties but excludes states having open primaries. See Appendix B, note 10.

* Denotes years in which party had incumbent President seeking re-election.

ocratic preference for the presidential primary as a means of candidate selection, i.e., numbers of contests, but to a greater escalation of mass involvement in the process itself—a notable response among a partisan electorate that has traditionally participated at a lower rate than Republicans in election politics.

Overall, what the data show is that both increases in the number of seriously contested primaries and in the turnout rates of rank and file party voters have occurred in recent nomination campaigns at the same time that turnout in the general election has been declining.[8] Popular presidential competition between the parties has apparently diminished during this period in spite of the highly politicized atmosphere of the 1960s and early 1970s, while popular intra-party competition has substantially increased—significantly and disproportionately within the Democratic Party.

8.   A note of caution must be interjected. General election turnout percentages are based on all eligible individuals, whereas primary voters are drawn from a pool of only those individuals already registered; therefore the *absolute* percentages are not directly comparable.

THE EXPANSION OF INTRA-PARTY CONFLICT

Besides the factors of a vastly differing composition of elite-types in the two parties and the preference of Democratic elites for popular conflict, other factors have also tended to exacerbate further the internal tensions in the Democratic Party and encourage intense primary election competition. As cited earlier, rapid declines in the support levels of traditional electoral core groups have stimulated new elites to test their strength against established party activists in open primary competition, encouraged by the uncertainty and instability of internal power relationships. In the Democratic Party of the last decade or so there has been no wing of the party that even closely approximates the overwhelming strength of the combined labor/organization power in the 1940s, 50s, and early 60s, and therefore a realistic chance for nomination exists for any candidate who can mobilize a sufficient base of support in a crowded field. The McGovern nomination campaign in 1972 clearly demonstrated both the weakness of established party elites in popular competition as well as the fragmented basis of the centrist elements of the party.

In addition to the substantive discontent (at both the mass and elite levels) housed within the Democratic "Sun," the development of strategic campaign weapons that enable a candidate to wage internal warfare have been vastly improved and contribute to the escalation of intensity in a party of divided factions. The development of television, for example, has provided the lesser-known challengers, shunned by established party leaders, with a quick and effective way to gain recognition among the party's mass electorate. And, as a result, the rapid development of modern communication technologies together with decline of patronage-supported organizational workers have shattered the near monopoly over campaign resources once maintained by local machines in primary competition. The modern campaign techniques have thus further reduced the "regular" organizational advantages, stimulated insurgent appetites, and simultaneously carried the spreading conflict to a larger and larger viewing audience.[9]

When one examines the recent trends, certain conclusions about the impact of television on participation in political elections are suggested. First, since participation in presidential general elections has declined in the last three elections, one could hardly claim that growing spectator interest has been translated into increased general election turnout. In contrast, participation in primary elections has sharply increased during the same period, both in total popular votes and in the rate of turnout. Thus in addition to previously cited sources of intra-party conflict, the development of "media politics," i.e., television, attitudinal research, demographics, etc., has apparently had a much greater impact on mass participation in intra-party contests than on the struggle between the two major parties. In terms of stimulating mass electoral responses to political conflict, the role of the media seems much more provocative of participation in nomination than in general election politics—particularly when aided by conflict-oriented elites.

Analysis of the data suggests that the media role can be explained in several ways. First, television itself produces a tremendous "multiplier" effect on conflict, spreading the scope and visibility of internal cleavages to great numbers of normally non-attentive partisans at large and arousing those who are concerned but inactive. Then, too, television's predilection for conflict and confrontation as a frequent definition of news events tends to accentuate internal differences, intensifying differences by dramatic exposure. Conflict, as Schattschneider observed, is likely to draw a crowd—on television as well as elsewhere—and the media's ability to extend the reach of provocative, challenging candidates is of critical importance in shaping the style and methods of insurgent campaigns.

9.   Saloma and Sontag noted that by the 1960s television was the most widely followed of the media and was also considered—by a wide margin—the most believable news source. *Parties,* p. 251.

Candidates of all kinds quite naturally vie to gain broad public exposure for their views, seeking to arouse the interest of those potential supporters who are their "primary public." In addition, the various supportive technologies widely utilized in campaigns—computers, attitudinal research, and highly professionalized software services—are used in conjunction with television to isolate and then strategically exploit the support of these special publics. In primary elections, then, the initial strategy of the successful candidate frequently becomes the opposite of the broad, aggregative and inclusive strategy required to build a majority in a general election. Essentially, the challenger, particularly in the early multi-candidate primaries, must first disaggregate or fragment the broad but often less intense support of the leading consensus-oriented candidates by isolating narrow but active clusters of support and then drawing these supporters to his candidacy. In pursuing this strategy, modern media-oriented technologies offer great potential, since computers, demographics, survey research, and the like all help in refining and identifying specific sub-strata of the party's rank and file.

Although these communication developments offer valuable strategic power for the lesser-known candidates, the usage of the media in primary elections has proved in the long run to be a mixed blessing. Television coverage of major primary campaigns can also dispose the general electorate to perceptions of the candidate that are hard to dissolve in the subsequent general election campaign. For example, the nationally televised Humphrey-McGovern debates during the 1972 California primary did much to weaken confidence in McGovern's economic proposals overall, when in response to persistent questioning he could offer no approximate cost estimate on his $1,000 per person welfare payment proposal. Though McGovern later stated, "I wish I had never heard of the goddam idea," millions of Americans in California and the nation were witnesses;[10] and for those who were not watch-

10.   Gary W. Hart, *Right From the Start: A Chronicle of the McGovern Campaign* (New York: Quadrangle, 1973), p. 190.

ing that day, Republican election commercials later in the campaign re-created the embarrassment of earlier Democratic divisions. Thus while there is little or no evidence that television has stimulated turnout in general elections, there are strong indications that television has added substantially to the overall scope and potential of popular intra-party conflict.

MAJORITY PARTY ELITES: CATALYSTS OF CONFLICT

In trying to understand why internal conflict has been increasing with singular focus in the majority party, a series of complex relationships must be considered. As Lubell pointed out in his "Sun-Moon" formulation, the majority party invariably houses more of the important political elements of society, and even though party victory and subsequent governmental power serves as a magnet holding these various interests together, the diversity of elements contained within the majority party also makes it more susceptible to friction stimulated by political inputs from inside and outside the majority coalition.

The greater heterogeneity of the Democratic Party coalition has, of course, been the subject of frequent examination. It has been noted that while both parties contain at least some supporters from most of the important electoral core groups, the Democrats draw from more disparate economic, religious, and racial interests.[11] The original base of the old New Deal coalition, the White working class, still prefers on balance to express its political interests through the Democratic Party, although the strength of its Democratic preference at the presidential level, as we have seen, has diminished substantially. In addition, a large percentage of the emerging middle class has aligned itself with the Democratic Party in the post-World War II period, along with a large majority of Black Americans who have linked themselves with the national

11.   See Axelrod, *op. cit.,* p. 140.

Democratic Party, largely ignoring (and being ignored by) the Republican Party.

The broader social range among mass groups favoring the Democratic Party conforms to Lubell's thesis of greater diversity in the majority party coalition. But while there are sources of potential conflict in the diversity of the majority party, it does not necessarily follow that mass electorates, relatively passive in terms of political activity, automatically increase their public participation in primary elections because of greater heterogeneity. What appears to be the critical factor linking potential to actual conflict is the dynamic interaction of elites in activist competition in the Democratic Party.

One need only look back at the last two sets of conventions to see key differences in the social bases and issue orientations among the activists of each party. In the Democratic conventions of 1968 and 1972, activists representing (or claiming to represent) labor, Blacks, the anti-war movement, urban machines, and party reformers were all joined in fierce competition—in marked contrast to the Republican conventions which, even without an incumbent in 1968, barely showed traces of such elite variety. What has apparently occurred is that while electoral groups in the mass (either social groups or "issue publics") generally have distributed themselves fairly broadly into both parties, *elites* leading these interests have not focused on both parties, preferring to work within one or the other party as far as designating party candidates and shaping policy platforms are concerned.

Thus, for example, while labor union voters have been split fairly evenly between the two parties for the last two decades, labor elites have worked almost exclusively through the Democratic Party in terms of party organizational activities and the nomination of the presidential candidate.[12] At the same time anti-war activists, Black activists, and "party reform" elites have also entered Democratic rather than Republican deliberations over presidential choices. As a result, the relationships of political elites within each

12.   See Greenstone, *op. cit.*, pp. 54–58.

party—the types, variety, and intensity of interaction—do not at all approximate the same broader proportions among rank and file party voters.

Herbert McClosky's study of the social and attitudinal differences between party activists at the 1956 national conventions and mass partisans at large indicated that in many ways party elites did not faithfully represent the rank and file voters of either party,[13] and in their follow-up of the McClosky study, Soule and Clarke found that similar distinctions between activists and followers were still strong at the 1968 conventions. Although the composition of the 1968 Democratic convention fell far short of the "representativeness" of the subsequent 1972 convention, Democratic Party elites still contained a much broader cross section of social and racial diversity than did Republican Party activists.[14]

But these differences between elites and mass publics do not explain why the Democratic Party has attracted such a diverse group of elites into its internal deliberations, even granting the fact that seeds of elite diversity are already present in the social diversity of the party's mass electorate. What are the factors that seemingly attract new racial, reformist, or "issue" activists disproportionately into the Democratic rather than the Republican Party, and hence further enlarge the scope and intensity of intra-party conflict? Most assuredly there is no single cause that can fully explain this circumstance, but one important reason appears to be that the inner circle of Democratic political decision-makers seems to be more easily penetrated by new elites; that is, the national Democratic Party organization has become internally a more "democratic" and more accessible organization—in marked con-

13.   See Herbert McClosky, Paul J. Hoffman, and Rosemary O'Hara, "Issue Conflict and Consensus Among Party Leaders and Followers," *American Political Science Review,* 54 (1960), 406–27.

14.   John W. Soule and James W. Clarke, "Issue Conflict and Consensus: A Comparative Study of Democratic and Republican Delegates to the 1968 National Conventions," *Journal of Politics,* 33 (1971), 72–91. In addition, the authors found Democratic elites far more fragmented on the important issues than Republicans by 1968.

trast to its party structure while the two-thirds rule was operative.

The encouraging of internal participation has not been fostered by the previously dominant labor/organization wing of the party, whose leaders have long preferred the oligarchic, stable, "brokerage" approach to party organizational activities from which they have profited. The pressure to open the party to even greater participation from new political interests has come rather from the increasingly active, middle and upper middle-class New Politics stratum of the Democratic Party, which has emerged as a vital and powerful force in increasing the accessibility of the party to certain new political elites.

While it has been shown that the affluent, college-educated strata of both parties are the most ideological segments of each,[15] the evidence of primary competition in each party (Tables 16 and 17) suggests that those ideologues who are "liberal" Democrats strongly favor broad-based intra-party democracy, while those who are "conservative" Republicans harbor more oligarchic attitudes toward party organization and intra-party popular participation. Thus the powerful ideological stratum in each of the two parties, the Democratic "amateur" and the Republican "purist," markedly differ in their attitudes toward encouraging new elites or the rank and file to participate in the internal processes of the party—with New Politics Democrats pressing to open their party to new mass-elite inputs in an atmosphere of procedural equality, while conservative "purists" in the Republican Party, as Kessel noted, tend to play down efforts to develop internal democracy through mass participation.[16]

15. See Everett Carll Ladd, Jr., and Charles D. Hadley, "Political Parties and Political Issues: Patterns and Differentiation since the New Deal," *op. cit.,* 44.
16. See John H. Kessel, *The Goldwater Coalition,* pp. 25–122. Kessel's analysis of the Goldwater "purist" faction details their problems with the primaries and their extraordinary success in the "brokerage" aspects of gaining delegates by state party conventions.
    Sydney Verba and Norman Nie have pointed out that the Republican Party houses the largest ideological segment of the two parties and also

There will, of course, be future exceptions to these elite predilections—the Republicans cannot continue to remain almost immune to the escalation of primary conflict—but increases in the relative scope of Republican primary competition will more probably develop from the strategic and symbolic needs of a particular "purist" candidate rather than from the acceptance by these same elites of the idea that the ultimate choice of a nominee *should be* made by a mass decision. While elite conflict may become intense as in 1964, there is much greater reluctance among those in the ideological wing of the Republican Party to expand the scope of internal conflict.

It seems clear that much of the growth in scope and intensity of mass conflict within the Democratic coalition can be attributed to the primary election orientation of New Politics elites, who have sought both to increase the policy content of the party and simultaneously to democratize the means for selecting the presidential candidate. In effect, the New Politics movement has pressed the party along two broad fronts of reform: first, for new, clear, substantive policy goals; second, for mass, internally democratic methods of selecting party candidates and policies.

These joint objectives stem essentially from a conception of American democracy held by many of the New Politics reformers. As James Q. Wilson noted in his analysis of an earlier model of the insurgent Democrat:

> The view held . . . implies that in a large and heterogeneous society the probability of government being "democratic" is increased significantly by political arrangements which broaden popular participation in the making of political decisions. Democracy, in this view, is the method for realizing the common good by allowing the people to decide issues through the

---

that these Republicans tend to be more active politically. However, the apparent lack of commitment by these elites to internal democracy seems to lessen the chances of activating the ideological commitment into mass involved intra-party conflict. See Sidney Verba and Norman H. Nie, *Participation in America: Political Democracy and Social Equality* (New York: Harper and Row, 1972), pp. 224–28.

election of individuals who assemble to carry out the popular will. If this is the case, then clearly the selection of elective officials ideally must be as democratic as possible from the very first—i.e., the selection of candidates by political parties must be as democratic as the election of office holders by the voters . . . government will be more democratic because as many people as possible can participate in the choice of those candidates and the writing of those platforms.[17]

Mass intra-party participation in the candidate and platform process is seen, therefore, as opening the party to more policy content, since the choices of the mass population would not then be limited to only a "pre-selected" choice of two organizational party candidates. Thus the strategic thrust of the reform faction has been to increase the extent of popular participation in the party selection procedures, while simultaneously accentuating the policy orientation along sharply defined and consistent programmatic lines.[18] More people participating in the preliminary choice of candidates and more clearly defined programmatic choices offered by the party have thus been the joint goals of New Politics Democrats.

The McGovern-Fraser Committee reforms, for example, were a successful attempt (as a result of pressure from the dominant New Politics faction on the committee) to broaden both the base of popular participation and to standardize nationally the divergent, locally determined, and "undemocratic" methods of selecting delegates in the different states. The wide latitude granted state methods of delegate selection was sharply limited by the Democratic National Committee, the first successful attempt to standardize and democratize a party long intentionally decentralized in its authority and procedures. For the New Politics wing of the Democratic Party, ideologically consistent policies and popular democratic procedures in selecting a presidential candidate were inti-

---

17. James Q. Wilson, *The Amateur Democrat*, p. 342.
18. For other views of how democracy operationally functions, see Joseph A. Schumpeter, *Capitalism, Socialism and Democracy* (London: Allen and Unwin, 1954), p. 269, and Robert Dahl, *A Preface to Democratic Theory*, pp. 131–32.

mately linked as necessary joint objectives for the reshaping and reforming of the Democratic Party.

The first phase of party reform—developing a clearly defined policy party together with attendant responsibility for carrying out the specific political platforms once elected—has been long demanded as essential to the revitalization of American politics.[19] To make the party system more responsive, reformist critics have insisted, policy must be clearly articulated by each national party's platform and presidential choice, along with the promise that those in the President's congressional party, i.e., Senators and Representatives, will implement those policies with their votes on specific legislation.

There are, nevertheless, at least two prerequisites for such an orderly transfer of political ideas into concrete policy legislation. First, the party members representing the individual states and regions must agree on what Democratic or Republican policy actually is, i.e., agree on the "meaning" of the party symbol; and second, if there is defection from an agreed upon national policy by recalcitrant members of the congressional party, the President, as the principal leader of national party policy (or his party deputy), must have some means of disciplining or ultimately removing them. Without the ability to limit the independent power of individual members of the House or Senate, and to remove them if they continue to vote counter to national policy, it is not possible to carry out consistent policies and maintain responsible party government.

In terms of the first requisite, consistency in the meaning of the party's symbol regarding specific issue orientations, one need only refer to the major differences found earlier between senatorial candidates in the same party on the social welfare liberalism and racial liberalism scales (Tables 11 and 12) to see that large differences in the meaning of the party symbol are not limited only to distinctions between "Southern" and "Northern" Democrats. In-

19. See particularly the American Political Science Association, Committee on Political Parties, "Toward a More Responsible Two-Party System," *American Political Science Review*, 44 (September 1950), Supplement.

deed, successful Republican senatorial candidates also sharply differ even within the confines of the urbanized regions of the East and Midwest, and differ to such an extent that the successful Eastern Republican candidates are much closer in policy terms to Eastern Democrats than they are to their fellow Republicans in the Midwest on the two most critical domestic issue spectra—social welfare activism and racial policy. As a result of the differences in the meaning of party symbols, consistent congressional policy in these two areas requires substantial inter-party agreement, not simply party cohesiveness.

Beyond the crucial regional difficulties of shaping consistent, clear-cut national policy parties, there remains, even if reasonable consistency could finally be developed, the very limited sanctions available to a national party leader to maintain necessary national party loyalty to these policies. If, for example, centrally agreed upon policy legislation is rejected by a member of the President's congressional party, what national party power can be brought to bear to replace that Congressman when the nominating party constituency is itself local rather than national?

Even granting the willingness of a local organization to subordinate itself to national party concerns,[20] local party organizations themselves are by no means powerful enough to win challenges for the party's designation consistently when they are carried into primary elections. It is, in fact, the primary election itself, the *sine qua non* of intra-party democracy, that has substantially limited the further development of any national organizational discipline over local "deviates," for if the electorate is to be offered a clear choice of policies, it is apparent that the party must be held responsible for the legislative actions of its congressional members. But a party without the national structural power to influence the

20. See Cornelius P. Cotter and Bernard C. Hennessy, *Politics Without Power: The National Party Committees* (New York: Atherton, 1964). For an interesting analysis of local party organization power relationships, see Samuel J. Eldersweld, *Political Parties: A Behavioral Analysis* (Chicago: Rand McNally, 1964), pp. 98–117.

naming of the candidate, and without the resources to resist the primary challenges of non-conforming Congressmen, cannot fulfill a national party mandate.[21]

As a result, a critical contradiction of objectives prevailing within the New Politics faction of the Democratic Party becomes clear: intra-party democracy by means of plebiscitarian candidate nominations in primary elections is sought, and, at the same time, the party is supposed to present clear, consistent and effective programs to the electorate at large.[22] Policy government requires party discipline which can provide the top echelons of the party with the power for controlling aberrant members. But party discipline and the elimination of organizationally destructive primaries conflicts with the reform wing's other objective of having popular, internally democratic contests to determine the party's candidate. In fact, even some of the staunchest early proponents of responsible party government, such as Schattschneider, did not propose to reform the parties along programmatic lines and simultaneously weaken party organizational control, as has been proposed by New Politics elites.

While a primary election is one potentially valuable means for shaping the choice of a party's candidate, its frequent use can be destructive to party organizational strength, leaving a party at the mercy of overly disruptive internal conflict. It does not follow that if *some* intra-party conflict is good to build and replenish leadership echelons, then *more* is even better. There are, of course, limits— difficult to define in practice—beyond which internal conflict becomes destructive. In addition, it also does not follow either logically or in practice that because primary elections can remove can-

21. The congressional party caucus does have sanctioning power over committee assignments, evidenced, for example, by the removal of several committee chairmen in 1975. However, the caucus is unable to control the naming of the local party candidates, and hence the vote of the Congressman.

22. See Austin Ranney, *The Doctrine of Responsible Party Government: Its Origins and Present State* (Urbana: University of Illinois Press, 1962), p. 13.

didates unresponsive to rank and file policy preferences, that those who are in fact victorious in primary elections necessarily reflect the policy views of the mass party electorate.

This can be clearly observed in non-presidential primaries, where the turnout of partisans often runs between 10 and 30 percent of the potential electorate, and victorious candidates often poll half or less of that shrunken turnout. How sure can we be that this "democratically" elected candidate represents a more genuine policy consensus of a party's rank and file than a candidate selected by a party organization, when so few take part in the decision-making process?

The analysis of candidate nominations in the earlier chapters has demonstrated quite clearly that the nominee at the state level does not necessarily reflect the political opinion of his rank and file partisans. The ability of Eastern Republican elites and their special publics to nominate liberal Republican candidates consistently offers ample evidence that political opinion can be distorted in the nominating process even with the availability of primary elections. Republican elites and their attentive publics, as noted earlier, were still able to nominate candidates who would not be selected if all Republicans had participated in the nomination process.

At the presidential level, primary election participation tends to run considerably higher (though each party maintains its own individual predilections) because of the greater saliency of the campaigns. However, even at this level, primaries do not result in a clear policy input by rank and file partisans, since many of the primaries are multi-candidate contests where less than 30 percent of those voting can bring victories, such as that won by McGovern in the 1972 Wisconsin primary.[23]

Lacking the two-candidate constraints of typical competition between the parties, intra-party elections are much more at the mercy of non-policy happenstance, such as the number of centrist

23. See Harry Zeidenstein, "Presidential Primaries—Reflections of the People's Choice?" *Journal of Politics,* 32 (November 1970), 856–74.

candidates competing for the same constituency and the number of liberal and conservative candidates seeking to represent their respective wings of the party. Indeed, much of McGovern's success in 1972 was due to the fragmenting of all but the left-liberal faction of the party as a result of the overlapping candidacies of Humphrey, Muskie, Jackson, and Wallace. Although the clear victor in primary contests in terms of delegates, McGovern did not even closely approach a majority mandate among Democrats who turned out, receiving about one out of every three votes in the fourteen states he ran in compared with the one out of three proportion gained by George Wallace in ten states.[24]

If primaries, then, are to serve a purpose in defining mass policy preferences for the national party, what policy positions can be deduced from these results? Clearly, McGovern did not represent a majority of Democratic voters, and yet his "minority" victory did gain him a 51 percent majority of *primary delegates,* playing by established "rules of the game."[25] The clear definition of party policy by "mass" participation in internally democratic primary elections appears, then, to go beyond the capability of American parties at present, both because of the narrow base of intra-party participation and the fragmenting effects of multi-candidate races.

The recent movement of the Democratic Party to a more plebiscitarian style of presidential nomination has not brought about a democratically defined political program but, rather, as the above-mentioned primary returns indicate, an increasingly wide range of policy preferences among Democrats. In effect, the elec-

24. Wallace gained many fewer delegates to the convention than the voting results would suggest, since he concentrated on the preferential aspect of the primaries and often did not file a full slate of delegates.

25. The mobilizing abilities of McGovern elites were just as impressive in gaining delegates by the caucus-convention method of selection. It is not true that they gained a widely disproportionate number in the initial caucuses. See Dennis G. Sullivan, Jeffrey L. Pressman, Benjamin I. Page, and John J. Lyons, *The Politics of Representation: The Democratic Convention 1972* (New York: St. Martin's Press, 1974), p. 19.

tion of approximately two out of three delegates to the Democratic national convention in 1972 only changed the relative power positions of different party elites, limiting the advantages of local party and labor elites (with low participation constituencies) and promoting the advantages of those nationally oriented, middle-class elites with more mobilizable supporters in primary elections. While the new rules of the game have encouraged greater mass participation and intra-party conflict, it is still far from clear that the choice of the candidate and party platform is any more reflective of the rank and file of the party than it has been in the past.

INTRA-PARTY CONFLICT:
A RESPONDING ELECTORATE

In recent years, electoral research has focused increasingly on the role of policy and ideology in the voting decisions of the American voter, reflecting the attempt to update an older image of the American voter. The old image of the American voting public, largely shaped by survey research undertaken during the decade from 1950 to 1960, showed Democratic and Republican rank and file without sharp differences in policy preferences in many areas, and with little consistency between one policy attitude and another. The systematic linking of one idea with other political attitudes— a requirement for genuine ideological thinking (belief constraints) —was identified as an important missing feature in the behavior of the American rank and file voter, in sharp contrast with the behavior of elites, e.g., business leaders, journalists, academicians, politicians, and professional leaders, whose attitudes on a series of important political issues were more highly intercorrelated.[26]

The research of Pomper, and more recently Nie and Andersen, has identified the static nature of those earlier findings which were based on the quiescent 1950s. Tracing attitudinal data over

26. See Campbell et al., *The American Voter,* and Converse, "The Nature of Belief Systems in Mass Publics," *loc. cit.*

time, their findings have demonstrated decisively that the perception of presidential candidates by the voters on the basis of issues has markedly increased and ideological constraints have been strengthened.[27] Since 1964, issues have become more highly correlated with the eventual presidential choice of the voter, reaching a much higher plateau of ideological consistency during the period of 1964 to 1972. As Nie and Andersen have summarized:

> In short, by 1972 we find substantial correlations between domestic and cold-war issues, strong relationships between positions on these issues and the attitudes on the civil liberties of dissenters, and a moderate to strong relationship between all these issues and the new social issues—indicating clearly a striking growth in the scope of the mass public's ideology as well as in its magnitude.[28]

It would be comforting if we could believe that the significant growth of issue consciousness and ideological consistency was the direct result of the two parties offering the electorate two defined sets of alternative programs and stimulating the voter, in a classical way, to a substantially higher level of political consciousness. It appears that at least some of the crystallization of issues has come from the conscious alternatives presented by the two parties, particularly on racial policies. But the thesis pursued here is that beyond the conscious efforts of *inter-party* differentiation, more of the growing policy awareness of the general electorate in the 1960s and early 1970s has been generated by unplanned intra-party conflict instead—primarily, but not exclusively, in the Democratic majority coalition.

In all three of the last presidential elections which encompassed this new policy-orientation plateau, intense and widespread intra-party conflict has surged through one or the other of the parties and appears to have served as a major catalyst in "ideologiz-

27. Pomper "From Confusion to Clarity," *loc. cit.,* Norman H. Nie with Kristi Andersen, "Mass Elite Systems Revisited: Political Change and Attitude Structure," *Journal of Politics,* 36 (August 1974), 540–87.
28. *Ibid.,* p. 564.

ing" the public at large. Here again we find the important political linkage between intra-party dynamics and mass publics, a linkage that points strongly to the fact that the growing consciousness of policy distinctions between the two parties' presidential choices is critically tied to intra-party elite decisions to do battle within the individual party.

The Democratic predilection for frequent primary battles and the vast number of voters participating in these conflicts has, in fact, played a critical role in sharpening the public's awareness of policy differentiation, linking by public exposure various issues, attitudes, and votes in a more consistent pattern. Another feature of recent nomination politics, the absence of highly attractive or charismatic presidential candidates in the last three elections, has also served to increase the ideological consistency of American politics by not blurring the issues through the mediating influence of the candidates' personal appeal.

The internal conflict that began with the Goldwater movement in the Republican Party in the early 1960s (with the provocative slogan, "a choice—not an echo") and then raged even more publicly among primary-prone Democrats in the late 1960s and the early 1970s, has ultimately served to educate the entire electorate in more ideological terms. Thus, a good case can be made that the major catalyst in stimulating greater mass distinctions of political policies has not come from conflict between the political elites and publics of the two major parties, i.e., after the nomination, but rather from the complex, intense, activist struggle before the parties' candidates have been chosen.

Elite conflict within the party has long existed, to which many tumultuous party conventions attest. But as intense and furious as conflict has been in the past, it has traditionally encompassed only a small part of the electorate in its struggles. In the past, party elites, most frequently local organizational leaders, fought and bargained with other elites to select the candidate, while at the same time the absence of overall public participation in the candidate selection process limited the extent to which conflict could be communicated to the rank and file party electorate. Reconciliation of mass party interests was not nearly as difficult after the nomination when only party elites were involved in intense intra-party conflict.

The marked increase in the scope and intensity of popular participation in recent years has, in effect, added many new policy cues that alert and direct voters in their ultimate choice in the *post-nomination* contest, thereby fulfilling the first objective of the Democratic reform movement, i.e., to increase the policy content of American party politics. But for the Democrats, the consequence of these new elite-stimulated ideological cues to the voter has been to divide the voters along policy lines that have produced electoral defeat by provoking sharp voter cleavages, particularly on racial and foreign policy, that are far less favorable than traditional partisan differences of socio-economic liberalism and conservatism.

Elites within the majority party must play, it appears, *two* dynamic linkage roles if the party is to gain the presidency: 1) coordinating the policies and publics *within* the party coalition, and 2) linking the intra-party universe to the political process of general election politics. Within the party, elites must stimulate sufficient conflict to ensure political progress, forcing the party to face the future as well as the past by keeping itself open to new political demands. At the same time they must also act as filters that defuse and deflect excessive conflict which threatens the viability of the party in the subsequent general election. Therefore, in order to be successful, elites active in party deliberations must of necessity link their activities to both the intra-party universe of nominations and to the subsequent general election universe of the entire voting population—objectives which are increasingly difficult to reconcile.

What makes this reconciliation increasingly difficult is not merely the spread in the number of primaries—presidential candidates have periodically opted for this kind of campaign in the past—but rather the growth of a *more direct and tightly bound relationship* between party elites and party mass followers. There is little doubt that television has played an important role in the tightening of this linkage, which has, in effect, narrowed the lee-way of elites in strategically building the necessary support in both the intra- and inter-party universes. For by enabling primary candidates to sharply define (and overdefine) their differences with other candidates of their party, both real and overprojected lines of internal policy conflict become indelibly drawn in the mind of the mass public.

The intensity, scope, and style of present Democratic Party competition seem to have become excessively disaggregative, fragmenting the support of traditional Democratic groups and over-burdening the internal system of a faltering old coalition—but without being able to establish a sufficient new one. The old internal elite structure, largely consisting of party organizational leaders, labor elites and appointed officials has been effectively shattered by primaries—but as yet no new elite structure has evolved that can effectively guide and channel the internal conflict of such disparate social, economic, and racial groups as are presently seeking expression within the Democratic Party.

The rapid shifting of electoral core support, the growing multiplicity of diverse activist corps, and the Democratic predilection for intense primary election conflict seems to have made the necessary coordination of the two "candidacy" universes exceedingly difficult. The disaggregative impact of intense intra-party competition has proven so far to be too resistant to later Democratic attempts to rebuild broad support in the subsequent general elections, leaving in the post-nomination aftermath an electorate more "educated" on policy but not favorable to the Democratic candidate after its stimulating but costly education.

8

Summary and Conclusions

What, then, has been revealed by this analysis of the dynamics of key electoral groups and political elites in the Democratic Party? First, we have found that suburbanization, as such, has not had a significant effect on the political ties of key urban Democratic groups that had migrated to the suburbs after World War II. Changes in party affiliation were very small in the suburbs in the critical regions of the East and Midwest, and, in addition, voting loyalty among transplanted urban Democrats was as high if not higher than that of Democrats remaining in the major cities.

Among Catholics and labor unionists, a paradoxical weakening of political ties to the Democratic Party was manifested in the East, where relatively liberal unionists and Catholics were more likely to affiliate with the Republican Party than their more conservative counterparts in the Midwest. The weakening in partisan loyalty among the more liberal Catholics and labor unionists in the East owed much to the relationship of the two parties in their respective regions. Republican Party elites in the East were found to have successfully reduced the normal Democratic advantage on liberal social welfare issues by nominating a succession of statewide Republican candidates who were much closer in their personal policy positions to the liberalism of Democratic candidates. By narrowing the candidate distance between Republican and Democratic nominees, the class basis of party politics was thus markedly reduced in the East, eliminating much of the anti-working-class, anti-social-welfare stigma attached to the symbol "Republican" and, in consequence, reshaping the symbol's meaning to operationally liberal Catholics and labor unionists in that region. As a result, when party conflict over social welfare issues was reduced by the similar candidate positions, group attachments to the Democratic Party overall were weakened, permitting Republican candidates to gain from conflict along new, more favorable lines of cleavage.

The important role of statewide party elites extended far beyond the impact of statewide candidacies on the pulling power of party symbols, since these same party elites were also involved in delegate competition to shape the national face of the party at the national convention. The eventual choice of the presidential nominee, and consequently the reaction of key groups in the electorate to that very choice, was found to involve state political elites at still another level of the party process, as national presidential candidacies had to be fought out in both state and national arenas.

The dynamics of mass/elite power relationships at the Democratic national convention were examined, where the party's successful presidential nominee both reflected internal power relationships and then, in turn, stimulated new reassessments by key groups in the subsequent general election. The internal instability of the Democratic Party was found to be both a response to the rapid changes in core support in the mass electorate as well as the result of elite stimulated conflict. Not only did major changes in mass support provoke elite conflict, but elite conflict itself stimulated the intensity and scope of subsequent *public* involvement in intraparty battles.

The weakening of labor and big city mass contributions to the Democratic coalition had apparently set the stage for challenges from new elite corps, particularly from reformist, issue-oriented activists of the New Politics wing of the party, who, in but a short period of time, had come to provide a disproportionate share of the mass mobilizing power within the party. These elites of the new middle class—culturally, rather than economically, middle class in outlook—were found to play a catalytic role in the escalation of public intra-party conflict by heavily promoting the ideological content of party politics and by simultaneously increasing the demand for primary-oriented internal democracy.

Affluent suburban Democrats were identified as an important part of the New Politics faction of the party, characteristically representing the broadening social basis of the post-World War II Democratic coalition. Although suburbanization itself was found to have had little influence on the voting loyalty of transplanted urban Democrats, its impact on intra-party affairs was nevertheless substantial, for besides the important financial and organizational resources provided by activists from the affluent suburbs, the suburbs themselves provided the New Politics wing with a strategic geo-political base. The combination of the intensity of suburban Democratic activists and the relative weakness of regular Democratic Party organizations in affluent suburbs offered an excellent political springboard from which the New Politics wing could contest opponents in primary election competition.

The dynamic interaction of mass and elite influence in the national Democratic Party was also examined from another perspective, focusing on the development and expression of racial conflict within the party after the restrictive two-thirds convention rule was removed. The change in the "rules of the game" was found to have stimulated new strategic calculations in the years following World War II, as Harry S. Truman sought to make race a national rather than a regional issue and gain needed support among Northern Black and civil rights groups in 1948. While the post-Truman years brought attempts to pacify the Southern wing of the party, the Supreme Court's *Brown* decision in 1954 ultimately forced clear-cut decisions of implementation on party leaders. Thus, when

John Kennedy and Lyndon Johnson followed through with a series of executive actions and legislation designed to alleviate racial inequities, the Democratic Party became clearly identified with the more liberal position on race.

Analysis of emergent Black party elites suggested that they would make a greater input in future Democratic Party conflict than had been made in the past, perhaps becoming a pivotal factor in intra-party battles. In prior convention conflict, Black party activists were found to be consistently allied with their most sympathetic audience, reformist liberals, as they jointly fought against those party procedures which restricted Black as well as insurgent White participation. However, the Black alliance with reform interests, though of proven effectiveness in the short run, was likely to be less solid over the long term. The greatest weakness of this alliance over time appearing to lie in the willingness of many in the New Politics wing to risk defeat in the general election as a price of political principle, whereas for Black elites, the relatively unprotected socio-economic position of their rank and file makes Democratic defeat in the general election far less acceptable even in the short run. The tentative economic position of Black masses in America, particularly when compared with that of their relatively affluent New Politics allies, suggested serious constraints on future Black alliances where ideological commitments might threaten immediate rank and file gains.

While the development of internal conflict has permeated the entire party system, interestingly and most importantly the scope of mass instability was not found to be equally shared by both parties, since substantial increases in both the number of contested primaries and in the rates of rank and file turnout were lodged primarily in the Democratic Party. The nature and mix of majority party elites were identified as a critical source of this mass-involved intra-party conflict, which has deeply penetrated the nomination process. In particular, reform pressure to enlarge the scope of public participation in the nomination process was found to have successfully shattered the old elite superstructure in the Democratic

Party, but without providing in the new rules of the game an adequate means by which internal conflict could be channeled and strategically managed so that the eventual Democratic nominee might successfully link the two universes of presidential candidacy.

THE DEMOCRATS AND THE FUTURE OF THE AMERICAN PARTY SYSTEM

The increasing scope and intensity of mass conflict within the majority party have been found to be critically linked to the weakening of the traditional urban core of the Democratic Party. The old majority coalition, basically dependent on White working-class and ethnic support in the urban regions of the North, has been weakened to the extent that, despite gains among Black and middle-class Whites, it has been able to win the presidency for only eight of the last twenty-four years.

In response to the clashing interests already established in the coalition and to those new claimants seeking to express themselves through the Democratic Party, destablizing conflict has spread through the party, leaving in its aftermath a disappointed middle-class reform movement, a disaffected White working class, and a Black under-class most materially deprived by the loss of Democratic presidential power. And continuing divisions within the party at the mass and elite levels suggest that long-term presidential leadership will be difficult to sustain, even though recent political and economic events will most probably work to the short-term advantage of the Democrats.[1]

The single most threatening division among the Democrats,

1. Also in the absence of a dominant presidential candidate in 1976, the new proportional representation rules presently in force at the Democratic convention will probably tend to promote "favorite son" candidacies. These rules will unintentionally serve to increase the "brokerage" input at the convention since it is less likely for one candidate to be close to gaining a majority through the primaries and thus possibly ease internal conflict in the near-term.

one that has cut deeply into Democratic urban strength, has been the fragmenting force of racial conflict, a cleavage which has split American society by violence and suppression from the nation's origins. In the long term, Democratic success in re-establishing a majority coalition will almost certainly be constrained by racial conflict between Blacks and Whites in the major cities of the North. To the extent that *broadly shared* economic and social welfare concerns dominate the agenda of American politics, i.e., operational liberalism cleavages, serious conflict over school busing, housing, "welfare," and other racially loaded issues will tend to remain localized and not rapidly shift upward through the federal system. But to the degree that economic stability and prosperity returns, Black and liberal White pressure for specific racial gains will of necessity provoke angry responses from those White Democrats most threatened by economic and social change in the major cities, and thus further destabilize the urban base of the party.

While a few large states of the West and Southwest, e.g., California and Texas, may in fact help to tip the balance in future close elections, Democratic chances for victory will probably be limited unless a solid base is maintained in those areas with substantial numbers of normally supportive working-class and Catholic populations.[2] Therefore, until significant headway can be made in assuaging local racial conflict among Whites and Blacks in the critical urban regions of the North, the Democrats will remain a deeply vulnerable and unstable coalition.

While the presidential future of the Democrats is clouded by its internal divisions, the likelihood of the Republican Party becoming a majority "Sun" party has been substantially reduced by the Watergate debacle and, more importantly, by the pronounced failure of the "business party" to keep the business of the economy under adequate control. However, even before these two most re-

2. It should be noted that while California has been an important state in intra-party conflict, the state's contribution to the Democratic presidential coalition in the past has been minimal. With the exception of the Johnson landslide in 1964, it has not gone Democratic since 1948.

cent blows to Republican hopes, the American electorate, though often permitting Republican Presidents to check the excesses of prior Democratic administrations, has been reluctant to give the Republicans simultaneous policy control of both the Congress and the presidency. Whereas the Democrats have gained several periods of joint control over Congress and the presidency with which to attempt the broad formulation of national policy, the Republicans, on the other hand, have been largely forced to remain a secondary "Moon" party, revolving around issues stimulated by Democrats, often profiting from Democratic activist failures, but unable to put together a broad, sustaining coalition behind their own party agenda. While Republican criticism of "big government" has generally found favor as an abstract idea (ideological conservatism), Republican efforts to shrink the specific socio-economic programs that underpin "big government" have not found similar approval from the mass electorate.

Taking the two parties together, prospects for a critical realignment of the party system seem unpromising. Instead, repeated wide swings between the parties—indicative of dealignment in presidential voting—appear to be the more probable outcome in future presidential competition. The growth in the scope of internal conflict together with the weakening of partisan loyalty in the electorate as a whole seems to have further encouraged wide swings among tentative electoral groups, whose voting decisions increasingly reflect the internal struggles of the parties. Consequently, the outcome of intra-party dynamics, primarily but not exclusively focused in Democratic nomination politics, will most probably be the key determinant of the direction and frequency of future swings between the presidential parties.

In this process, majority party elites interacting with their mass publics will play a critical role in achieving (or failing to achieve) an acceptable balance of conflict and reconciliation within the party, one that will enable the party's nominee to link the universes of nomination and general election politics. And it seems likely that the price of a successful linkage is a significant reduction in rank and file involvement in the nomination process, limiting the scope and intensity of direct democracy in the selection of the party's candidate.

The difficult problems facing party elites in this critical task of internal conflict resolution have, in fact, substantially increased in just the past decade or two. Particularly for the Democratic Party, the entire nomination process has become more penetrable by outside political pressure as the organizing ability of discontented forces in American society has markedly improved, and new claimants, social groups, and issue publics, have sought out the party system for redress. As the more accessible and "democratic" party, the national Democratic Party has disproportionately felt this pressure, and the overload on the internal structure of the party has contributed to frequent presidential defeats.

The development of such a direct and tightly bound relationship between party elites and mass followers among Democrats—indicated by both the escalation in the number of competitive primaries and sharp increases in rank and file turnout—severely narrows the subsequent leeway needed for elites to link intra-party and inter-party universes, and consequently makes the path to the White House far more difficult for the Democrats. But does it follow, then, that the Democratic Party reforms of the past decade that opened the party to more equitable participation have also irreparably weakened the Democratic Party? A cautious answer to this question is "No, not necessarily," for the "opening" of the party—making it more accessible to competing groups of activists—does not necessarily require a major increase in *mass* intra-party conflict. An open party does not necessarily mean a party of frequent and intense primary elections.

While a certain number of primaries—substantially fewer than available at present—can be a valuable testing ground for the candidate, in terms of a party successfully linking both the intra-party and inter-party electorates, it is the establishment and maintenance of fair and open non-primary procedures that is most critical. Non-primary procedures, *providing that they remain open and equi-*

table, can permit new interests in the mass electorate to penetrate the party leadership level, while contributing relatively little disaggregating influence on a necessarily broad internal consensus. As a result, a better balance of direct and indirect democracy within the party may be established, permitting elites to play their critical linkage role effectively, a role which has been substantially circumscribed by plebiscitarian democracy.

The intensity of conflict within the Republican Party should not be underestimated either—in all likelihood it will follow the trends already perceived among Democrats. However, the critical distinctions between the two parties in terms of conflict at the present do not lie simply in the intensity of elite feelings on issues or in activist combativeness at the national conventions, as Republican conventions attest, but, rather, in the willingness and ability of Democrat elites to enlarge the scope of partisan involvement in the nomination process.

In a sense, the problems facing Democratic leadership elites—activists and candidates—in resolving excessive socio-political claims reflect the inadequacy of the two parties to aggregate and express a satisfactory range of choices successfully, forcing back upon individual parties excessive political responsibilities which they are ill-suited to manage. Lacking the aggregating channels of a dualist system, multi-candidate primary elections disaggregate internal power and distort the results of conflict at the very moment they open the range of intra-party choice, and consequently restrict general election chances. Attempts to increase the socialization of conflict by expanding the range of choice within one party are not at all sound substitutes for *socializing inter-party conflict,* for they do not define alternative choices in such a way that the mass public can properly grasp the elements of decision and render judgment.

The framing of the choices is, then, a critical function—or obligation—of political elites and not the responsibility of a diffuse mass party electorate, since it is only in response to elite formulation of the political complexities that the electorate can intelligently exercise its right of decision. The responsibility for improving the limited capacity of the party system to serve American democracy is thus intimately involved, as Key has observed, with the attitudes and capabilities of those who are the opinion leaders and activists in the political structure, who serve both as *catalysts and filters* of political conflict.

But the difficulties encountered by party elites in their task of properly shaping political choices cannot be underestimated, for they face problems that are far more taxing than those faced by party leaders only two decades ago. The rapid development of competing political groups to challenge "regular" party authority, the step-level growth in the number and force of hitherto unorganized claimant groups, and the increased volatility of media-oriented political opinion have all added substantial disaggregating pressures that work against the reconciliation of internal party demands.

Historically, the parties have served as blunt instruments of political expression, often sluggish in response and working best in periods where crisis and outstanding political leadership have galvanized the system. But today the political demands of various clientele groups have become more intense and differentiated in focus, and expectations of immediate outputs have rapidly risen— all at the same time that the resources needed by party leaders to reconcile and synthesize conflicting interests effectively have shrunk. In short, the sweep of social change has made major new demands on a party system that is unaccustomed to speed, differentiation, and ideology, producing as a result the dynamics of an impatient body politic in a party system demanding patience.

For the Democrats to stand a reasonable chance of successfully integrating old and new claimant in the same majority coalition, accessibility to party deliberations for a variety of political elites must be assured by the maintenance of fair and open non-primary procedures in the delegate selection process. But the scope and intensity of intra-party democracy must be significantly reduced by either formal or informal means, since excessive mass-involved conflict has confused and alienated the electorate, diminished the eventual candidate's chances for victory, and led to further declines in mass participation in the two-party process. If the Democratic Party does not remain accessible to new sociopolitical elites, it cannot weave the past into the future. But if it insists on maintaining the luxury of full-blown intra-party democracy, the long-term power of its voice will be muffled by the sounds of its own conflict, for while the disparate voices of mass factions need be heard, they cannot be substituted for that critical function of political leadership—shaping the choices of democracy.

APPENDIX A

TABLE 18. A Comparison of Registration and Self-identification Among Voters and Non-Voters in Midwestern and Eastern Suburbs (1968 Presidential Election)

	Registration of:		Identification of:	
	Voters	*Nonvoters*	*Voters*	*Nonvoters*
Midwest				
(Sample Sizes)	(188)	(111)	(235)	(110)
Democrat	49%	7%	37%	29%
Republican	36	4	28	20
Independent	15	5	33	31
Other/None	—	84	2	20
East				
(Sample Sizes)	(193)	(95)	(325)	(132)
Democrat	40%	12%	40%	37%
Republican	49	12	38	17
Independent	11	3	19	26
Other/None	—	73	3	20

Source: Harris Urban-Suburban Survey and Harris Suburban Survey

TABLE 19.   Socio-economic Status of Catholics and Protestants in Midwestern and Eastern Suburbs and Cities

Region	Midwest				East			
Socio-economic status	High	Me-dium	Low	(Sample Sizes)	High	Me-dium	Low	(Sample Sizes)
Catholics								
Suburbs	43%	50	7	(125)	31%	49	20	(245)
Cities	22%	51	27	(101)	14%	55	31	(128)
Protestants								
Suburbs	39%	40	22	(176)	30%	49	21	(145)
Cities	26%	54	20	(127)	51%	24	24	(49)[b]

Source: Harris Urban-Suburban Survey[a]
   [a] Blacks not included.
   [b] Small sample size.

TABLE 20.   Ethnicity of Catholics and Protestants in Midwestern and Eastern Suburbs

	Midwest		East	
	Catholics	Protestants	Catholics	Protestants
(Sample Sizes)	(107)	(164)	(149)	(119)
Ethnic[a]	49%	35%	70%	50%
Non-Ethnic	51	65	30	50

Source: Harris Suburban Survey
   [a] Ethnic defined as born in a foreign country, or one or both parents born outside U.S.A.

TABLE 21. 1968 Presidential Vote in Midwestern and Eastern Suburbs as a Joint Function of Socio-economic Status and Union Membership

	Midwest			East		
	Humphrey	Nixon	(Sample Sizes)	Humphrey	Nixon	(Sample Sizes)
Lower Socio-Economic Status	32%	35%	(161)	27%	41%	(140)
Union Members	48	24	(85)	35	37	(49)
Non-Union Members	13	47	(76)	23	43	(91)
Higher Socio-Economic Status	26%	59%	(104)	27%	56%	(120)
Union Members	40	36	(25)	31	48	(29)
Non-Union Members	22	66	(79)	25	58	(91)

Source: Harris Suburban Survey[a]

[a] Includes Protestant and Catholic White Union members only.

APPENDIX B
Methodology

1) The Harris Suburban Survey and the Harris Urban-Suburban Survey both control for the same geographic areas of the East and Midwest (i.e., the identical states) as well as the same metropolitan areas (150,000 population and over). One distinction should be noted: the definition of "suburb" is slightly different in the two surveys. The Harris Suburban Survey includes the entire non-urban part of the SMSA as "suburb," whereas the Harris Urban-Suburban Survey does not include the distant reaches of an adjacent county in the SMSA definition, including only the "urban-fringe" of a metropolitan area.

The SMSA definition weights the sample of "suburbs" with a slightly higher percentage of "small towns" than in the "urban fringe" definition and moderately increases the relative number of Protestants to Catholics. To avoid any methodological problem, we have not used any comparisons in the text between the suburban populations of the two surveys, even though the differences are small.

2) Comparison of the Harris Suburban Survey and the suburban section of the Harris Urban-Suburban Survey verified the regional differences in affiliation in the Midwest and East. Suburban migratory patterns, however, could only be obtained from the Harris Suburban Survey, since neither Harris, Gallup, nor Survey Research Center surveys regularly asked the respondent where he or she moved from (the question asked was usually, "where were you brought up," or "where were you born").

3) Three separate Harris surveys were combined to form the Harris Urban-Suburban Survey and were then retabulated to conform to the same limitations of the retabulated Harris Suburban Survey, i.e., the same regional definitions and size of central cities (150,000).

4) Fred I. Greenstein and Raymond Wolfinger, using 1952 and 1956 presidential data, concluded that suburban residence may well produce Republican converts,[1] while Manis and Stine came to the contrasting conclusion that suburban residence seems to be politically irrelevant.[2] Millet and Pittman's research on the suburbs of Rochester, New York, could find no evidence that suburban living brought a trend to Republicanism,[3] while Lazerwitz's study of suburban voting between 1948 and 1956, detected a drift toward the Democrats.[4] Scott Greer's voting survey of Catholics in metropolitan St. Louis showed that Catholics still gave sub-

1. Fred I. Greenstein and Raymond H. Wolfinger, "The Suburbs and Shifting Party Loyalties," *Public Opinion Quarterly*, XXII, 4 (Winter 1958–59), 473–82.

2. Jerome G. Manis and Leo C. Stine, "Suburban Residence and Political Behavior," *Public Opinion Quarterly*, XXII, 4 (Winter 1958–59), 483–89.

3. John H. Millet and David Pittman, "The New Suburban Voter: A Case Study in Electoral Behavior," *Southwestern Social Science Quarterly*, XXXIX, 1 (June 1958), 33–42.

4. Bernard Lazerwitz, "Suburban Voting Trends: 1948 to 1956," *Social Forces*, XXXIX, 1 (October 1960), 29–36.

stantial majorities to the Democrats, but that class for class there were still more Republican votes in suburbs than in the city itself.[5]

5)   Scaling of Socio-Economic Status (SES) of Harris Suburban Survey. Socio-Economic Status in the Harris Suburban Survey was based on four variables: education, income, occupation, and house value (or rent). The procedure was to obtain a score for each individual on each variable, and the sum of these scores was then used to classify the individuals as either *high* or *low* SES. The scoring procedure was as follows:

SES VARIABLE

Education	Score	Income	Score
0-8 years	1	Under $5,000	1
Some high school	2	$5,000-$9,999	2
High school graduate		$10,000-$14,999	3
or some college	3	$15,000-$19,999	4
College graduate	4	$20,000 or more	5
Post-graduate	5		

Occupation	Score	House Value (or Rental)	Score
Unskilled worker	1	Under $10,000 (under $100)	1
Skilled worker	2	$10,000-$19,999 ($100-$199)	2
Service/clerical	3	$20,000-$24,999 ($200-$249)	3
Sales/manager	4	$25,000-$49,999 ($250-$299)	4
Professional/		$50,000-($300-)	5
technical	5		

Summing an individual's scores for the four variables resulted in a distribution of total scores ranging from a mimimum of 4 to a maximum of 20. Individuals with total scores ranging from 4 through 11 were categorized as *low* SES, while those with total scores ranging from 12 through 20 were categorized as *high* SES.

5.   Scott Greer, "Catholic Voters and the Democratic Party," *Public Opinion Quarterly*, XXV, 3 (Fall 1961), 611–25.

6) An individual's score value on the Racial Liberalism Scale could range from 0 to 5 depending upon how many of the following five statements he answered with a pro-Black response.

 a) "Some people say that the government in Washington should see to it that White and Negro children are allowed to go to the same schools. Others claim this is not the government's business." Do you think the government in Washington should . . .

 b) As you know, Congress passed a bill that Negroes should have a right to go to any hotel or restaurant they can afford, just like anybody else. Some people feel that this is something the government in Washington should support.

 c) Some say that the civil rights people have been trying to push too fast. Others feel they haven't pushed fast enough. How about you: do you think that civil rights leaders are trying to push too fast, are going too slowly, or are they moving about the right speed?

 d) Which of these statements do you agree with: 1) White people have a right to keep Negroes out of their neighborhoods if they want to. 2) Negroes have a right to live wherever they can afford to, just like anyone else.

 e) What about you? Are you in favor of desegregation, strict segregation, or something in between?

7) Sample sizes for Operational Liberalism and Ideological Liberalism scales.

OPERATIONAL SCALE

	Rep.	Dem.	Ind.	Prot.	Cath.	Un.	Non-Un.
Midwest:	231	277	231	580	141	235	514
East:	217	297	162	279	283	167	520

IDEOLOGICAL SCALE

	Rep.	Dem.	Ind.	Prot.	Cath.	Un.	Non-Un.
Midwest:	111	150	111	288	79	119	258
East:	118	156	84	150	139	90	276

8)   Racial Roll Calls and Scoring. Determined by Americans for Democratic Action position as the liberal position.

ADA
Position

1964

HR 7152. Acceptance of Mansfield (D., Mont.) motion   Y
to table point of order to refer House-passed civil Rights
bill to Senate Judiciary Committee.

Adoption of Mansfield (D., Mont.)–Dirksen (R., Ill.)   Y
motion that the Senate invoke cloture on the Southern
filibuster on the Civil Rights Act.

Rejection of Russell (D., Ga.) amendment to HR 7152   Y
to postpone the effectiveness of the public accommoda-
tions section until Nov. 15, 1965.

Rejection of Ervin (D., N.C.) amendment to HR 7152   Y
to limit authority of individual Equal Employment Opportunities Commission members to file discrimination
charges and initiate investigations concerning job discrimination.

1968

HR 2516. Civil Rights-Open Housing. Mansfield (D.,   Y
Mont.) motion to invoke cloture on the pending Dirksen
(R., Ill.) amendment to provide open housing requirements as well as penalties for interference with speci-
fied civil rights.

HR 2516. Baker (R., Tenn.) amendment to exempt from   N
the coverage of the pending Dirksen (R., Ill.) amendment's open housing provisions any single-family owner-
occupied house sold or rented through a real-estate
broker or agent if the owner did not instruct the broker
to discriminate or indicate to him an intent to discriminate.

1969

HR 13111. Labor–HEW Appropriations. Scott (R., Pa.)   Y
amendment adding "except as required by the Constitution" to school desegregation provisions.

1970

HR 514. Elementary and Secondary Education Amend-   N
ments. Stennis amendment requiring equal enforcement
throughout the country in dealing with *de jure* and *de
facto* school segregation.

HR 15931. Labor–HEW Appropriations. Mathias (R.,   Y
Md.) amendment adding "except as required by the
Constitution" to school desegregation provision barring
use of funds to go beyond freedom of choice.

Nomination of G. Harrold Carswell as an Associate Jus-   N
tice of the Supreme Court.

S 2453. Equal Employment Opportunities Enforcement   N
Act amendment, Dominick (R., Colo.), providing for
enforcement of equal employment opportunity in federal
district courts rather than through cease-and-desist
orders.

1972

S 2515. Equal Employment Opportunities Enforcement.   N
Dominick (R., Colo.) amendment, as amended by Javits
(R., N.Y.) and Beall (R., Md.) amendments, to substi-
tute (for a provision in the bill authorizing the EEOC to
issue cease-and-desist orders to discriminatory employers) language allowing the EEOC to take recalcitrant
discriminatory employers to federal district courts for
enforcement of equal job opportunity.

S 659. Omnibus Education Amendments of 1972. Griffin   N
(R., Mich.) amendment to Allen (D., Ala.) amendment
barring federal courts from ordering busing of school
children on the basis of race, color, religion, or national
origin and forbidding the withholding of federal aid to
induce implementation of busing plans.

S 659. Higher Education Amendments of 1972. Adop-   N
tion of the conference report (S Rept. 92-798) authorizing $19-billion for higher education programs through
fiscal 1975 and $2 billion for school desegregation aid
through fiscal 1974, establishing a new program of direct

federal aid to needy students and containing compromise
provisions postponing implementation of court orders requiring busing of school children.

HR 13915. Equal Educational Opportunities. Proxmire   N
(D., Wis.) motion to invoke cloture on the bill containing strong busing limits.

RACIAL LIBERALISM

EAST Democrats	Total Civil Right Issues Voted	Total Vote for Issues	Total Vote against Issues	Racial Liberalism Score
Dodd	9	9	0	100
Ribicoff	15	14	1	93
Kennedy	14	14	0	100
Williams	15	13	2	86
Clark	6	5	1	83
Pastore	14	11	3	78
Pell	15	13	2	86
MIDWEST *Democrats*				
Stevenson	4	3	1	75
Douglas	4	4	0	100
Bayh	14	13	1	92
Hartke	12	12	0	100
Hart	15	15	0	100
McNamara	4	4	0	100
Lausche	6	3	3	50
Young	11	11	0	100
Nelson	14	10	4	71
Proxmire	15	12	3	80
EAST *Republicans*				
Brooke	11	11	0	100
Weicker	4	3	1	75
Saltonstall	4	4	0	100
Case	15	15	0	100
Javits	15	15	0	100

Keating	4	4	0	100
Scott	15	12	3	80
Schweiker	9	7	2	77
Goodell	4	4	0	100
Buckley	4	1	3	25

MIDWEST
Republicans

Percy	11	10	1	90
Dirksen	6	4	2	66
Griffin	11	5	6	45
Saxbe	8	3	5	37
Taft	3	1	2	33

An individual's racial liberalism score (%) was obtained by dividing each individual's total support for civil rights issues by the total number of racial issues voted. Thus:

$$\text{R.L. } (\%) = \frac{\text{Total Civil Rights Support}}{\text{Total Racial Issues Voted}}$$

9) "Racially liberal" was defined by a score of 3, 4, or 5 on the Racial Liberalism Scale. "Racially conservative" was defined by a score of 0, 1, or 2 on the Racial Liberalism Scale.

10)   Presidential Primaries in Selected States
Republican turnout in presidential primaries, by state, among those states maintaining party registration figures in percentages.

STATE	1948	1952	1956	1960	1964	1968	1972
Calif.	44	71	59	60	75	46	73
Mass.	11*	50	7	7	14	19	23
Neb.	—	—	—	—	—	61	53
N.H.	—	—	—	—	—	64	66
N.M.	—	—	—	—	—	—	13
Ore.	70	69	59	62	75	73	60
Pa.	9	37	33	37	17	11	7
S.D.	—	—	—	—	—	48	27
W.Va.	29	39*	27*	31*	32	NP	NP

Democratic turnout in presidential primaries, by state, among those states maintaining party registration figures, in percentages.

STATE	1948	1952	1956	1960	1964	1968	1972
Calif.	30	55	60	54	62	72	80
Mass.	8*	7	7	16	8	22	52
Neb.	—	—	—	—	—	56	60
N.H.	—	—	—	—	—	54	69
N.M.	—	—	—	—	—	—	48
Ore.	40	52	43	68	60	68	62
Pa.	19	8	33	10	9	23	46
S.D.	—	—	—	—	—	63	18
W.Va.	24	28*	17*	58	NP	NP	55

— Indicates those years without registration figures.
NP Indicates years in which no primary was held.
 * Indicates primaries but without presidential preference.

Index

DATE DUE
